# The Keys to God's Storehouse

## Daily/Weekly Meditations, Bible Study and Scriptures

## By: Louise Manigault

### www.myinspirationsfromgod.com

*Cover Design: Mr. Martin Reyes*
*mrreyes2@juno.com*

ISBN-10: 146640406X
EAN-13: 9781466404069
LCCN: 2011918025
CreateSpace, North Charleston, SC

# THE KEYS TO GOD'S STOREHOUSE

## Table of Contents

## Section Three – Bible Study Devotions . . . . . . . . . . . . . . 85

# Introduction

My mother used to keep a wardrobe closet in my bed-room. I knew there were valuable items of clothing and other artifacts in there, but she always kept it locked. The closet required two keys, one for each door. When she passed away, I looked for the keys among her things. She had lots of keys, and I tried quite a few before I found the right ones. When I opened it, I found all kinds of treasure, things that were precious to my mother. She had several fur coats, some antique jewelry and some porcelain dolls that she had received when she was a child. At first, I wanted to keep the wardrobe locked and not share the contents, but then I realized that some of the items would be a blessing for other family members who wanted to have a keepsake to remember my mother.

God also keeps a storehouse. There are more blessings than we can count in His storehouse, and He wants us to have access. He wants us to find the keys that will open the doors to the abundance that He has stored up for us. We can gain access to God's storehouse by living a life led by the Spirit. The keys that will open

God's storehouse are found in the New Testament Book of Galatians, chapter 5, verse 22: "love, joy, peace, patience, kindness, goodness, faithfulness, gentleness and self control."

If you choose to live a life that does not conform to the fruits of the Spirit, your life will be ruled by worry, fear, anxiety, doubts and unfaithfulness to God's will for you. This storehouse of misery is not the one we should want to open. It contains burdens and not blessings. It contains situations that will bring the pains and heartaches of life. There is no joy in this storehouse.

Each of the inspirations, in this new book, is designed to help you open the door to God's storehouse of blessings. In this storehouse, you will receive the keys for an abundant, fulfilling life through prayer, meditation and the study of God's word through Bible study and the scriptures. In this storehouse, you will gain the understanding and wisdom which tells you to, *"Take heart! I have overcome the world."* Unless otherwise noted, all scriptures are taken from the NIV Bible.

*Louise Manigault*

# Section One: Daily Meditations

**Sunday**
**The Foundation for a Good Life**
Love has to be the foundation of your life. If you are not acting out of love, you will always feel uneasy, anxious and unfulfilled. When your life is guided by love, you will be compassionate and forgiving. You will stop holding onto the negatives. You will always release your anger and move forward to claim your blessings. Life will be worth living when you remember that God is love, and His love is the foundation for a good life.

**Monday**
**Proceed with Passion**
Many people go through life following routines that are less than exciting to them. Everyday is the same thing, morning to night. There is no real excitement or joy about anything. If you want to live a happy life, you must do the things that truly make you happy. You have to pursue the goals and dreams that fuel your passion, and then your life will be full of joy.

## Tuesday
## Turn Pain into Purpose

When we are hurt by someone or a situation, we tend to allow it to consume us. We can't function or move forward because the pain is blocking us. You can use your experience to help someone else by sharing in a small group. You can use your situation to create something new and exciting. Passion and purpose comes as a result of the things that you have learned.

## Wednesday
## Take Time to Relax Your Mind.

We often work and overwork our minds during stressful, anxious times, and yet we force ourselves to keep going on to the next task without taking some time to allow our minds to recover. Take a few minutes to get away from the routine and the stresses each day. Go outside or find a peaceful place, and let your mind float to something pleasant and even funny. Do something silly to make yourself laugh. Take some deep breaths and release the tension. A few relaxing minutes each day will make a difference in your emotional state of mind.

## Thursday
## Go With the Flow

The flow of the Universe cannot be stopped or slowed. It keeps going no matter what is happening around us. As the song says, "Hold to God's unchanging hand... Build your hopes on things eternal." If we do that, we will get through any situation. Nothing will defeat us. Enjoy today; be at peace and don't miss out on the joy of the day by worrying about tomorrow!

## Friday
## Fill 'er Up

It's absolutely possible to fill your mind with positive thoughts no matter what your circumstances may be. It's possible to find peace in the midst of chaos. You can see beyond the negatives to find the source of your power. Trust God more. Fill up on His words for your life.

## Saturday
## Keep Your Focus on Faith

The late Rev. Dorothy Carrington Benjamin wrote about Faith in the Foreword of one of my books. She said: *"As Christians, we have been taught to hold fast to our faith during the bad news days. Faith is what we want to hold onto in the midst of a health crisis, a financial struggle or a tragic loss. Keeping our Focus on Faith on painful days is our only guarantee that we will get through those days with strength, confidence and hope for a new day."*

## Sunday
## Broken Hearts Heal

Each time we are involved in a friendship or romantic relationship, there is a possibility that our hearts will be broken. People disappoint us and hurt us. The important thing to remember is that our broken hearts will heal. We have to recognize that people are in our lives for a season and a reason. There is a lesson to learn, and an opportunity to grow in wisdom and understanding. Even though it seems like the end of the world, it is not. Trust in the healing power of your spirit and have faith that God will bring you something better than you lost. Stay in the flow of God's blessings and know that He will bring you the blessings that you seek.

**Monday**
**Build Your Confidence**
When we pray to God and ask Him to hear and answer our petitions, we can have more confidence and faith by remembering all of the prayers that God has answered in the past. Remember how He reversed situations, brought the miracles and made a way even when things seemed impossible. When you remember and express gratitude for what God has done, you will be more confident about what He will do for you now and in the future. You can be at peace because you know that God will never let you down.

**Tuesday**
**God's Love Never Changes**
There are many things that change in our lives. People come and go; relationships change; we change, but we can always count on God and His steadfast love for us. We can have confidence in His promise to bring us through our trials and tests. We can be sure that He loves us unconditionally. When you can't depend on other people, always know that you can depend on God.

**Wednesday**
**Don't Doubt God's Power**
Even when things are going against you, God's says, "no weapon formed against you will succeed." (Isaiah 54:17) We are confronted with evil everyday. Sometimes, we are not even aware that there are people who want to hurt or destroy us. God has the power to protect you from what is seen and what is unseen.

**Thursday**
**Don't Put God on Hold**

While we are busy struggling with issues and concerns, God is calling us. He is trying to reach us with the answer, but we always put Him on hold. We think that we know the answer, that we have the solution. It's only after we have tried and failed over and over that we finally remember that God is waiting for us to acknowledge His presence.

**Friday**
**Peace of Mind**

There are things that we can sacrifice in our lives, but we cannot live without peace of mind. In order to reach that state of mind, we must pray everyday and stay in the word by a daily reading of the scriptures. As the word becomes rooted in your mind and spirit, it forces out the fear, anxiety and stress. You will find clarity and peace of mind.

**Saturday**
**Are You Missing Out?**

How many times have you allowed the perfect opportunity to pass you by? We allow opportunities for success to go by because we are afraid to take a risk. We have doubts about our ability to engage ourselves in a new venture. We spend too much time analyzing and over evaluating a situation. We tell ourselves that the opportunity will be there when we finish a few things that we are doing. We convince ourselves that time will stand still until we are ready to make a move. The truth is, time keeps moving and those opportunities are passing by at a faster and faster rate. You are getting older, and the chance for something new and exciting is getting further and further away. Step out on faith, and God will take two steps for you.

## Sunday
### Cherish the Moments

Sometimes it may seem that our lives stretch out endlessly like the horizon, but in reality, we are a tiny part of the universe, here for a short time in the grand scheme of things. It is important for us to cherish every moment. Find some enjoyment in each day. Let go of the grudges and unforgiveness. Do something nice for someone. Do something nice for yourself. Follow your passions and your dreams. Thank God for your life, and live it to the fullest. Trust God to make a way to take care of the things that you cannot.

## Monday
### Take a Holy Moment

Everything in your day is going wrong. You've had arguments with friends and family. Every turn is the wrong direction. It's time to take a holy moment with God. Confess to Him those things that cause you to feel weak and powerless in your life. Ask Him to come into your life and restore your peace and joy. God loves you and wants you to have a close personal relationship with Him. When life is going wrong, and you can't seem to find your way, take a holy moment and spend some quiet time with God.

**Tuesday**
**Living Within**

There may be times that we don't feel that God is near to us, but God wants you to know that you do exist within Him. You are a part of Him. His spirit lives within you, and when you are hurting, God feels your pain. He knows your deepest feelings and what you need. He will respond and bring comfort and relief. God's love for you never changes. It doesn't matter how far you go, you cannot escape from God. His compassion will always reach out to surround you.

**Wednesday**
**Plan Ahead**

When we are in the midst of trials and tests, it takes all of your time and drains your energy. No matter what is going on, you still have to plan for the time when you will be restored. God does not stop planning for your future blessings and victories. He has paved the way and set the stage.

**Thursday**
**Evil Cannot Win**

The scripture says, "In this world there will be troubles, but take heart! I have overcome the world." (John 16:33) When we are being assaulted by situations and circumstances on a daily basis, it is hard to believe that we can overcome, but God's word tells us that He will overcome evil and give us the victory. If you have faith and believe in God's power, your prayers will be answered. Good will overcome evil if you trust and believe God.

**Friday**
**Be Alert for the Rescue**
There is a favorite story that some pastors tell about the man who was caught in a flood and ended up on the roof of his house waiting for rescue. He kept saying that God would save him, but he drowned because he refused every offer to help him. When he met God and inquired as to why he was allowed to die, God told him that he had sent help, but he kept refusing. When we are struggling and drowning in a sea of troubles, God is coming to the rescue. Be alert and look for His deliverance.

**Saturday**
**Cleanse Your Spirit Daily**
If nothing is working in your life, perhaps you are blocking your blessings with negative thoughts. What we think and say directly impacts the things that come into our lives. If you are continually thinking about the worst, the worst will show up. Confusion, anxiety and fear will always be in control. You can cleanse your spirit by beginning your day with prayer and reading some scriptures. Reinforce your faith and belief in God to bring the miracles.

**Sunday**
**Renew Your Commitment**
As children of God, we are not always obedient to His word. There are times when we run amok. We stay away from worship services; we don't read the Bible or pray as often as we should. We allow jealousy to control our actions toward others, and we act out of hate instead of

love. Remember your faith foundation. Return to God and renew your commitment to be faithful to His plans for your life.

## Monday
## You Can Overcome

Life is a series of ups and down. When we are in the down times, we can feel overwhelmed with fears, worries and anxiety. We may feel that a negative situation has pushed all of the hope far beyond our reach. It seems like the dark will last forever. You must remember and believe that God knows your pain. He knows what you need. He will not abandon you. God will bring you through. He will help you to overcome.

## Tuesday
## The Path to God's Blessings

If you really want to be closer to God, you must commit to daily prayers. When you are in prayer, your words open a connection between your spirit and the spirit of God. It opens you up to receive God's message to you. God wants us to come to Him so He can respond to our needs. When have finished praying, you will feel your soul opening up to receive the blessings.

## Wednesday
## Put the Pedal to the Metal

There is nothing more frustrating than riding in a car with someone who drives 20 miles below the speed limit. Not that we want them to speed, but it would be nice if they could at least keep with the posted speed and the flow of traffic. Instead, they are traveling leisurely down the road while other cars are blowing their horns and whizzing by. Sometimes you want to tell them to let you drive because you want to get to your destination before the event is over! If your friends are creeping along below the speed limit of life, tell them to put the pedal to the metal!

**Thursday**
**Keep Moving**
Tough times have always come and gone. Sometimes things that you think will work, don't work at all. Sometimes you build your hopes up only to be disappointed. Plans fail; people fail you. It is important to remember that you are still a person loved and valued by God. Stop waiting for things to get better before you take action. God will always give you the strength to keep moving forward.

**Friday**
**Shake It Up**
Are you feeling bored with your life? Sometimes we get stuck in routines. We travel the same way to and from work. We sit in the same seats on the train or at church. We watch the same channels and TV shows. Doing the same thing, the same way, without much variation, leads to boredom and depression. Shake up your life. Change your closet around and find some different shoes and clothes to wear. Take a different route to work. Listen to some music instead of watching the same TV shows. Arrange your furniture a different way. A few changes will refresh your spirit and give you a different perspective

on life. Little changes can bring big results. Shake up your life today.

## Saturday
### Find Your Fortress of Solitude

How often do you have an opportunity to spend time with yourself? When you are at home, family, telephones, electronics, interruptions and disruptions ring in your ears all evening. At work, projects and tasks keep coming and going. Sometimes, you don't have a moment to think. Superman was a fictional character, but even he had a fortress of solitude. He went to that place when he needed time to think and regroup for his battles. We always need time to think and refocus. We need time to get back to our true selves. Find your fortress of solitude. Go there on a regular basis to refresh your spirit and regain your peace.

## Sunday
### Begin With God

If you want to feel more peace and less anxiety, begin your day with God. Read some scriptures with your cup of coffee. Pray to God, and ask Him to give you peace throughout the day. Seek His protection as you travel. Ask Him to lead and guide you in your work and conversations. Your day will be less stressful and more joy-filled.

## Monday
### Respect Yourself

You cannot command respect from others until you learn to respect yourself. You have to love yourself before someone else can love you. You have to be good to yourself if you want other people to be good to you. You cannot expect other people to give you what you are not willing and able to give to yourself. You have to set the example, and others will follow your lead, and if they don't, walk away from them.

**Tuesday**
**Express Your Gratitude**
When everything is wrong and your day seems dark and dreary, take some time to express your gratitude to God. Make a list, in your journal, of all the blessings you have received from God. Write about the trials that God turned into triumphs. Count your blessings instead of your burdens. Gratitude opens your heart and spirit to receive more blessings from God. Take time to express your gratitude every day.

**Wednesday**
**A Random Act of Kindness**
When you are feeling down, go out and perform an act of kindness for someone. Visit the elderly or the sick and shut-in. Make calls to people you have not spoken to in a while. Buy a small gift for someone, just because. Each time you perform an act of kindness, it makes you smile; it gives you a warm feeling; it takes your mind off your troubles for a while. By the time you return home, you will feel more hopeful. While you are helping someone else, God is helping you. Random acts of kindness flow in a circle leading back to you.

## Thursday
## Forget New Year's Resolutions

People make resolutions at the beginning of the year that are lost in the trash in a few weeks. Try something different. Set your goals from birthday to birthday. Evaluate where you are during your birthday week, and then decide what you would like to accomplish by your next birthday. As you get closer and closer to the next birthday, you will evaluate and make adjustments to keep yourself on target. Plan a reward for the goals accomplished by your next birthday. That will be a real celebration of life!

## Friday
## Spend Time with the Family

Families are pulled in many different directions. Children are playing computer games, watching television or talking and texting; parents are working late or on part time jobs, bringing work home and running to different meetings. Everyone is doing their thing. What has happened to the family unit? Designate specific days and times when the family will be together without any of the distractions. Sit down at the dining room table for dinner. Share the events of the day. Plan a family outing. Spend time with your children, or they will spend time with the wrong people. Spend time with your spouse, or they will seek comfort elsewhere. Togetherness is everything when it comes to the family.

## Saturday
### God Will Catch You

When we were children, we used to play a game where one person had to blindfold themselves. Another person would stand behind them. The blindfolded person had to fall back and trust that the other person would catch them. If someone wanted to be mean, they would not catch the person until the last second or let them fall all the way down. When we trust people to catch us or be there for us, we are often disappointed, but you can be sure that God will always catch you when you fall. He will not leave you alone or turn His back on you. You can trust God to catch you every time.

## Sunday
### Reinforcements and Protection

Soldiers don't go into battle without protective gear and the assurance that there are reinforcements coming to help with the battle. Worship provides the reinforcements and protection that we need to win the daily battle of life. The preached word arms us with strength to face the world. It reassures us that God is on our side and that He is our strength and shield.

## Monday
### My Way, or Else!

Sometimes couples get into terrible arguments that escalate until one of the parties issues an ultimatum: "It's my way or the highway." How devastating it can be if the other partner opts for the highway. In the heat of anger, we often say things that we don't really mean. We are in a bad mood, and our objectivity is blinded by our stubbornness. When two tornadoes collide, you can count on destruction. Both parties are destroyed by words that cannot be taken back. Before you lash out in anger, take a time out. Allow yourselves to cool down, and then commit to having a calm talk about the situation. Listen, really listen to each other. Sometimes, the highway may be the only viable solution, but that decision cannot be made during the height of your anger.

**Tuesday**
**Don't Carry a Grudge to the Grave**
Sometimes anger and frustration over a situation can cause you to walk away from a friend or family member vowing never to speak to them again. As the years pass, you grow further apart. Stubbornness and pride won't allow either side to take a step toward reconciliation. No one wants to say "I'm sorry." You may realize, when it's too late, you should have taken steps to overcome and makeup. Don't carry a grudge to the grave.

**Wednesday**
**Fix What Doesn't Work**
We often force ourselves to live with situations and people that cause us heartache and pain. If something is not working in your life, you can fix it. It may require a complete change in your life in order to restore your peace of mind. You may have to make adjustments or seek a total separation. Either way, you have to stop being a martyr in your own life. Evaluate your situation; make a decision, and then take action.

## Thursday
## Happiness is Found Inside

People search high and low for things and other people who will make them feel happy and fulfilled. They buy things every time they feel bored, depressed or lonely. They look to their relationships to make them happy. They put the burden on others to be responsible for this impossible task, but no matter how much they do, it is never enough for long lasting happiness. You have to look inside to find your real happiness. When you succeed, nothing on the outside will disturb it.


## Friday
## Release Yourself From Past Mistakes

We often spend time thinking about our past mistakes and what we should have or could have done differently. We agonize over things that we did to disappoint ourselves and others. We wish we could go back and do some things differently. We should not spend time beating ourselves up for what we did or didn't do. We cannot worry about the paths we should have taken. Whatever our pasts have been, we should be thankful because those paths have brought us to where we are today. Beginning now, we can make better choices for our future.


## Saturday
## Enjoy Yourself

Do you have friends and relatives who plan every minute of their vacation? From the moment the trip is booked, they begin to micro-manage something that should be fun. They have to be sure the hotel is exactly as they requested. They have to plan when and where they will go throughout each day and evening of the trip. They make a fuss about anything that changes their meticulous plan. One unfortunate incident ruins their entire trip, and they spend every minute complaining about what happened.

The object of the trip is "vacation". After booking the flight and the hotel, make an allowance for spontaneity. Enjoy being away from time clocks and routines. Let your spirit flow free, and enjoy your vacation. After all, that's why you're taking one in the first place!

**Sunday**
**Too Busy to Pray?**
We are busy people: too busy to return phone calls; too busy to write an email or letter; too busy to pay a visit to someone who is sick and shut-in. We are too busy to get to worship, and too busy to pray. What happens when we are in the midst of a trial? We want God to help us right away. We want instant relief. Suppose God said, "You were too busy to spend time with me, so I'm too busy to answer your prayer!" Make time in the morning and time in the evening to pray. Spend time with God. He is worth the effort.

**Monday**
**Don't Let Satan Run Your Life**
When you allow negative thoughts and behaviors to rule your life, you open the door to Satan. When he gets into your life, he will wreak havoc with your thinking and your actions. He will convince you that what is right is wrong. He will control your thinking and cause you to

say and do hurtful things to people. He will send you down a path that leads to more heartache and pain. He will keep you in a state of confusion and agitation. He will take full advantage of you when you are in a low mood. Stay in prayer. Ask God to lead you. Ask Him to fix you. Ask God to show you the way. Every time you pray and read the scriptures, you force Satan to flee from you, and when he does, the clouds will clear, and you will see your life in a positive light.

## Tuesday
## Don't Burn Your Bridges

When you are living a negative life, you hurt the people who are closest to you. You push away the people who are trying to help you. You burn the bridges that connect you to the people that you need in your life, and then you discover that you are cut off and alone. Cross the bridge and reach out to the people who love and care about you. Use the bridge to bring you closer and leave the negative emotions on the other side. Your life will get better if you don't burn your bridges.

## Wednesday
## Nothing is too Hard for God

Whenever pain or heartache, troubles or fears, overwhelm you, take it to God. Put it on the altar. Ask Him to come into your life right now. Ask Him to touch you, heal you and make you whole again. Ask Him to shower you with His grace and mercy. Keep believing and trusting God even when things look impossible. He will make a move that you have not anticipated.

**Thursday**
**Don't Get Caught up in the Drama**
We get caught up in the business of the day, and too often, our goals and plans get lost in the shuffle. We are drawn away from the things that we want to do for ourselves because we have to deal with the drama of friends and relatives. All the while, time and days are passing us by, causing us to lose control of our lives. Don't allow everyone's drama to keep you from the doing the things that you want to do to improve your life and further your goals. You have a plan. Stick to it.

**Friday**
**Have a Get Together**
In almost every city, there are places called Social Clubs where people can get together to drink, dance and have fun with their friends and make new acquaintances. People look forward to the opportunities at the end of a stressful work week. Have you ever considered having a get together to pray when life's trials and struggles are beating you down? Invite a few friends to your house for prayer time. When two or three are gathered together for prayer, God is always present.

**Saturday**
**The Power of One Word**
One word will help you to relieve most of your stress and anxiety. One word will free up your time to do the things that really matter to you. One word will make you victorious in every situation. That word is **"No."** How many times are you drawn into situations that you really don't like just because you could not say no? How many

times are you stuck going places that you don't want to go because you could not say no? How many times has guilt forced you to go along when you really wanted to say no? When people know that it is difficult for you to say no, they will always take advantage of you. Take back your power. Learn how to say "No!"

**Sunday**
**Are You a Basket Case?**
Your mind is not at peace when you don't get enough rest and you're in worry mode all the time. Add to these the fact that you're running yourself ragged trying to keep up with the demands of your job and family obligations. All of these things are draining your energy. Stop and take a break before you make yourself sick.

**Monday**
**God Works in Mysterious Ways**
Have you ever thought about someone you haven't seen for a long time, and all of a sudden, they call? Have you ever had one plan and a thought said, "do this instead," and it led you to a blessing for someone else and you, too? We are always bewildered when these events take place. Some attribute it to coincidence, but others believe that it is the work of God moving in our lives. It may not be in our plan, but it is in God's plan.

**Tuesday**
**Expect Some Detours**
Wouldn't it be nice if we could travel a smooth path along life's highway? Unfortunately, the reality is there will be

detours, pot holes and ditches to maneuver around. God has not promised us a smooth ride, but He has promised a victorious arrival. "In this world, you will have troubles and trials, but take heart. I have overcome the world."

**Wednesday**
**God Will Touch Someone's Heart**
There are people who are not very nice to us. They welcome every opportunity to say or do something to hurt us. No matter what we do or say, they refuse our attempts at reconciliation. We finally give up and begin to stay away from them in order to protect our peace of mind. Even though we stay away, we should not stop praying for God to touch their hearts and minds. God can and will work miracles.

**Thursday**
**You can Push Past the Barriers**
Sometimes people can go along, day after day, year after year, getting things done, tackling projects, reaching goals, being everything to everyone, and then it happens. The day comes when you get up and you don't feel like doing anything for yourself or anyone else. Your energy has deserted you. You're just going through the motions – trying to make it through the day. You're not really sick, but you are sick and tired. As they say, "your get up and go, got up and went!" You've hit a brick wall with your energy and mental drive, and you don't know how to get beyond the barriers.

It will require extra prayer time with God to regain your strength and determination. It will also require some changes in your daily routines and associations with people and organizations that no longer fit into your life. You can and will refresh your spirit when you find a new focus for your mental and physical energy.

## Friday
### Confidence is the Key to Achievement

People who have confidence will always find a way to achieve their dreams. Confidence in yourself and your desire to reach your goals will always keep you moving forward. You will not give in to worry and fear. You will not be stopped by temporary failures. You will learn from your mistakes, make adjustments and continue to move forward. If you have confidence, negative people will not deflect you. They will empower you to succeed because they don't think that you can. Maintain confidence and faith in God to move you from good to great.

## Saturday
### Love is the Key to Peace

As children of God, we have a responsibility to operate in love as expressed in 1 Corinthians 13:4-8, summarized as follows: "Love is patient and kind. It is not proud, rude or self-seeking...It always protects, trusts, hopes and perseveres. Love never fails." If you follow the principles of love, your life will be filled with peace no matter what is going on around you. Love will always win because God is love!

**Sunday**
**Worship is the Key to Spiritual Growth**

Some people prefer to watch the television worship experiences with the various ministers who can be found on different channels on a variety of days and times. They believe they have received the word, and therefore, nothing else is necessary for their time with God, but there is more to the worship experience. When you attend worship, you are immersed in the total experience of communing with God. You are filled by the music, the prayers and the preached word. You are able to fellowship in the service with other believers. You can gather together for the prayers of the people to pray for common causes and yourself. You are in a sacred God space where you can feel surrounded by His presence and gain a better understanding of His will for your life.

# Section Two: Weekly Inspirational Readings

## -1-
## Do You Have a Melody?

There is a line in a current, popular song that says, "If you listen, there's a melody in how you live your life. You can write the song you want." (El-Debarge)

Life has a rhythm. It is not just a random set of occurrences. If you observe the behavior of people, you will begin to see the patterns or melodies that control their lives. Sometimes the melody changes, but it does not vary much from the dominant tune. Do you know your melody? Here are some of the observations I have noticed:

There are some who are always the rappers. They must talk about everything over and over again, day in and day out. They replay the tune until you become exhausted from hearing it. If you listen close enough and long enough, their words begin to rhyme.

There are the smooth operators. They always have a "line." They want to say something that is sure to get your attention, and before you know it, they have convinced you to do what they want you to do or smooth-talked you into believing they are sincere.

You have the people who sing the blues. Life is sad. People don't treat them right. They are always singing a chorus of heart break hotel. None of their relationships work out. They are constantly crying the blues about all of their situations. They sing those songs until you start to feel the blues with them.

Some people remind you of a heavy metal band. Nothing they say makes much sense, but they will overpower everyone with their noise. They are determined to out argue everyone by being the loudest and most obnoxious person in the group. They have to be heard.

Don't forget the oldies but goodies group. They love the past more than the present. They can sing all day long about their lives 30, 40 or 50 years ago. It was the best of times, even though it may have actually been the worst of times for them. If you have only five minutes to spend with them, they will find a way to quickly take you back to the good 'ole days.

I'm sure you know people who sing these melodies and more. Their melodies are their stories. They may have some variation, but they are the same. You will smile as you fit them into the melodies of life. What melodies are you playing? Would you like to change them or add to them? You decide.

# -2-
# I Recommend God

When potential candidates for ordination apply through our denomination, one of the requirements is to obtain 3 letters of recommendation from people who know them and can attest to their character and worthiness.

Those letters talk about how long they have known the candidate and some of the good things the candidate has done that makes him or her worthy to be an ordained minister. Some of the letters make reference to the commitment of the candidate to do good works as a minister of God's people.

When some of your friends and family are going through difficult times, they need a recommendation from you. They need a letter of reference telling them how God can be the One who will bring them comfort and peace.

When you recommend that they try God, give them some scriptures to confirm your recommendations.

"Delight yourself in the Lord, and He will give you the desires of your heart." (Psalm 37:4)

## -3-
## Thy Will be Done

Do you sometimes wonder if God really answers prayer? There are times that we pray to overcome certain situations and trials that we are facing, and yet, it seems that God does not hear us because nothing happens. It seems like God has temporarily abandoned us in our time of need.

The Psalmist (Psalm 88) calls on God in his despair, and yet he says that God has not heard or answered his prayers for relief. In the book of Job, Job was plagued by one devastation after another. He kept praying to God for relief, but bad things kept happening to him.

In this world of people wanting instant answers and quick fixes, we expect God to respond to our needs the same way. We forget one important line in the Lord's Prayer: "Thy will be done." God answers our prayers, but the answer may not come as fast as we want or be the answer that we expect. How often do we pray for one thing this week, change our minds the next week and pray for something else. The fact is, God sees the whole picture of our lives while we only see a small part. When we pray and ask God for something, we cannot see that the answered prayer may lead to more trouble down the line for us.

Pauline thought she had met the perfect man after many years of searching. Tim was the nicest man she had ever met. He was good to her. He wined and dined her and bought her all kinds of expensive gifts. She was really in love, and she kept praying that they would get married. She thought her prayers had been answered when Tim popped the question. She wanted to get married right away, but they could not get the date that she wanted for the wedding. They had to wait for several months before they could get married.

As the wedding day approached, Pauline began to notice a few small things about Tim that didn't match with the great person she thought he was. She saw several displays of an angry temperament that began to frighten her. It made her begin to have second thoughts about this "perfect man" she was about to marry. She began to pay close attention to his behavior, and she finally realized Tim was not the man for her. She canceled the wedding. When she told Tim, he flew into a rage and stormed out. She was shaking because she was afraid that he was going to hit her. She had never experienced that type of relationship. She thought God had answered her prayer when Tim came into her life, but then she realized that the delay in the date was really an answer from God. He used the time to reveal Tim's true nature which saved Pauline from a doomed marriage. She thanked God for doing His will.

As we pray, we should always remember to add, "Thy will be done on earth as it is in heaven." The things of this world are temporary, conflicting and confusing, always changing like shifting winds, but God's will is perfect. James 1:17 says, "Every good and perfect gift is from above, coming down from the Father of the heavenly light, who does not change like shifting shadows."

Have faith in God to answer your prayers according to His perfect will. Remember, Lamentations 3:25-26, "The Lord is good to those whose hope is in him, to the one who seeks him; it is good to wait quietly for the salvation of the Lord."

# -4-
# Be Willing to Do the Work

Consider these scenarios:

**1.** Sherry and Terrell were sweethearts in college. Everyone thought they were the perfect couple. When Terrell asked Sherry to marry him, it was a dream come true. They planned the perfect wedding. It was going to be a fairytale day. Sherry wanted everyone they knew to be a part of this special day. The catering hall was secured; the church was chosen. The whole day was perfect. Everyone was happy, and the couple was swept up in the fantasy. Their honeymoon was lavish and expensive.

The next month, reality began to set in. They now had to face the bills and the loan that was secured to pay for their wedding. Even though Sherry and Terrell had decent jobs, the expenses from the wedding put a severe strain on their budget. They struggled to meet their obligations each month. Terrell soon learned that Sherry was not good with taking care of finances. She continued to spend more than they could afford. He also found out that Sherry was a terrible housekeeper. She didn't like to cook or wash dishes. Most of their meals were take-out, and Terrell spent much of his time off from work doing the cleaning. They spent most of their time arguing about everything. Terrell was fed up. He began staying out late after work and sometimes did not return until the next day. After six months, their fairytale had turned into a nightmare. They were not willing to do the work, and their marriage fell apart.

**2.** Monique was always overweight. When she was in school, her so called friends teased her all the time. She was always depressed about her situation. Her only escape was reading. She liked to read all of the fashion magazines and dream about the day she would look like some of the models she admired.

She promised herself that she would work to lose weight and get in shape. Each week, she told herself that she would begin her new healthy eating plan. She went to a nutritionist who worked with her to develop a sound nutritional program. Monique signed up for a one year program at a local gym. She began her day feeling positive, but by the time she came home from work, she was tired and frustrated. She didn't feel like going to the gym, and she could not resist stopping at her favorite fast food spot for a high fat meal. As she sat on the sofa eating and watching her soap operas, she was back to her old habits. At the end of each evening, she promised herself that she would begin again next week. She ate what she wanted for the rest of the week and did not go to the gym. Days turned into weeks, and weeks turned into months. The result was Monique gained another 20 pounds. She could not do the work to take the weight off and get fit.

**3.** Sean began working as soon as he left high school. He got a job that was paying a decent salary, and he did not see any reason to go back to school. As the years passed, Sean saw many of the employees moving up through the company and earning better pay. Each year, at his job performance evaluation, the team told Sean that he was doing a decent job, but he had the potential to do more if he would go back to school for his degree.

Sean went home and checked colleges online. He received brochures and information about tuition and grants. He promised himself that he would begin by the Fall, but then other distractions took him away from his promise. The same thing happened with the Spring semester. He kept putting school off until one day, the human resources manager called him in to tell him that his position was being eliminated. She wanted to know if he had enrolled in school. She had other positions available, but he needed a degree. She was willing to put him into a new position on a probationary period if he was enrolled and working on his degree, but, unfortunately, Sean had not followed through on his plan to return to school. She had no choice. She terminated him. Sean kept making excuses for putting off the work, and now he was out of a job.

Some of these scenarios may fit you, or they may remind you of something in your life that is not the way you want it to be. Life is not easy. It is not a fairytale. At a Les Brown seminar, he said one thing that I always remember: "Life is a fight for territory. Once you stop fighting for what you want, what you don't want, takes over." What do you want for your life? What goals do you want to achieve? What do you want to change? In order to achieve success, happiness and fulfillment, you have to be willing to do the work!

## -5-
## Expand Your Mind

We read about these situations all the time:

1. The woman who lost over 100 pounds and then gained all of it back plus more.

2. The 5 Million Dollar Lottery winner who was bankrupt in 3 years and facing more debt than he had before.

3. The homeless, drug addicted man who was discovered by agencies and hired to be an announcer was back on the street and then in rehab after a few weeks of his new-found success.

4. The self-help author and motivational speaker who rose to the top and then lost everything in a few short years because she thought she was ready for the big time, but in reality, she was not.

What do all of these people have in common? Their outside circumstances went too far and fast beyond their internal beliefs. The outside success represented the champagne life, but inside, they were continuing to think on the level of beer and peanuts.

You cannot hope to achieve and retain lasting success if you continue to think in the same, limited way as you did before your accomplishments. You must be willing to do the mental work to expand your mind and your thinking. You cannot skip the necessary levels and expect to have a solid foundation to build on. Successful people have different levels of mental energy, and with every step toward success, they work to expand themselves and prepare themselves for the challenges that success will bring. If your mental energy does not change, you will not be able to sustain your success. You will collapse and lose your desire to keep moving in a positive direction, and then, you will move backward faster than you moved forward.

Here are several things that you can do to prepare yourself, mentally, for success.

1. You have to be fully committed to what you want to do. You cannot work on your goal today and then procrastinate for a few weeks before you do anything else. You know that you have to go to work everyday if you want to keep your job. You have to be willing to make the same commitment to yourself and your goals.

2. You need to make a list of the negative habits that have been holding you back, and then begin working on a plan to eliminate those habits. You cannot change them all at once. You have to work on one at a time. It takes at least 3 weeks to begin to see the change that you want, and you cannot give up if you have an occasional set back.

3. You must constantly challenge yourself to do better. With every success, you will gain strength, courage and wisdom.

4. Be realistic. Success does not come overnight. You have to be patient and accept the fact that there will be setbacks.

5. Read authors who have achieved their dreams of success. Study their methods, and use the ones that fit into your goals.

6. Make time each day to clear your head and meditate. It is important to stay focused. Think about what you want to achieve; visualize yourself being successful.

7. Find a mentor who has been successful in a similar career. They will help you to avoid some of the mistakes and make suggestions that will help you move forward. They will motivate you when you are stalled.

8. Stay away from and stop sharing your plans with negative people. They do not want you to succeed, and they will find ways to discourage you and block your way.

These are a few of the things you can do to expand and then maintain your mental energy. Believe in yourself and stay positive. Don't be discouraged by the small setbacks. Keep moving forward. You will reach your goals if you do not give up!

## -6-
# Do You Have a Plan?

I would like for you to take a minute to think about where you were in your life last year at this time and where you are today. If you are satisfied with the progress that you have made, then you should keep going, but if you find that you have not achieved most of your goals or advanced your life, it's time to stop and re-evaluate your plan.

Of course, the first question you should answer is - Do you have a plan? Some people live each day just hoping for the best, but not doing anything to affect the outcome or results. Many of us live everyday with unhappiness, disappointment and frustration because we feel powerless to do what it takes to make life better for ourselves. Sometimes, fear prevents us from moving forward.

If you don't want to feel dissatisfied when your next birthday rolls around, you are going to have to take some action now to change some things. What will it take to make you happy? It may seem beyond your reach, but if you begin to take some small steps now, you will be pleasantly surprised with the progress you have made by your next birthday.

Martin Luther King, Jr., said, "Take one step in faith. You don't have to see the whole staircase. Just take one step." As you plan your journey this year, stay faithful in prayer and believe that God can and will make a way.

Don't look at what is. Have faith in what you cannot yet see. God sees the whole picture, and we have to trust that He will not lead us in the wrong direction.

Here are some scriptures to reassure you of God's power in your life:

"If God is for us, who can be against us?" (Romans 8:31b)

"Greater is He that is in you than he that is in the world" (1 John 4:4(KJV)

"No weapon formed against you shall prosper." (Isaiah 54:17 (KJV)

"See I am doing a new thing...I am making a way in the desert and streams in the wasteland." (Isaiah 43:18-19)

"Yes, from ancient days I am he. No one can deliver out of my hand. When I act, who can reverse it?" (Isaiah 43:13)

"What you decide on will be done, and light will shine on your way." (Job 22:28)

These scriptures will give you the power to move forward to achieve everything that your heart desires. Read them whenever you start to doubt. Trust God. His love for us never fails.

# -7-
# Stop Holding Yourself Back

Every year we begin with the thought that we are going to do better and live better than we did the year before. It sounds like a great plan until a challenge or test begins to block us from the things that we want to do.

You must remember that the life you live is based on the choices you make. You can choose to let challenges hold you back, or you can decide to work through them.

Challenges are not meant to stop us, but to make us stronger and more determined. Make your plan, chart your course, and don't let anything stop you from reaching your destination. Remember the success that you are seeking is right on the other side of your challenge.

# -8-
# Time to Get Back on Track

People do a lot of soul-searching in the beginning months of the year. They look back over the months and days of the previous year and think about the events, goals accomplished and things left undone. Some people feel a sense of accomplishment and look forward to doing bigger and better things this year, but many others feel a sense of guilt because they have fallen far short of their goals and dreams.

What has caused us to have feelings of regret?

1. We made excuses week after week for not working on our goals.

2. We allowed distractions to take our attention in different directions.

3. We spent too much time on toxic friends.

4. We watched too much television.

5. We wasted time on non-essential things.

6. We put everyone's demands ahead of our needs.

Unfortunately, last year was not the only time we allowed these things to happen. It has become a regular pattern year after year. It's easy to find excuses for abandoning your goals. It's easier than working on them. Anything that you want to accomplish will take hard work and commitment. You have to decide that you will not stop or give up no matter what happens around you.

Several things happen when you complete a goal. You feel good about yourself because you realize that you can accomplish the things that you set out to do. You feel motivated to begin another project. You find that you have developed your sense of self-discipline. You realize how many unimportant things and people were always standing in your way. You discover how much you learned about being organized in your work and thinking.

If you want to have a success-filled year, you must get back on track. You may have to stay up later at night or get up earlier in the morning. Set your goals and lay out your plan. Then get started and keep going. You will have more confidence in yourself. The rewards will be great, and your sense of fulfillment and accomplishment will bring on a new feeling of "I can do it!"

**-9-**
# The Rough Side of the Mountain.

John 16:33 "In this world you will have trouble, but take heart! I have overcome the world."

It seems that we spend our lives continuously climbing the rough side of the mountains. Do you wonder if there is ever a smooth path to follow to the top. Apparently there is not! But the wonderful thing about reaching the top of that mountain is being able to look back and see how you made it through. You didn't give up. You kept going until you reached the top.

What happens after we have reached the top and lingered awhile to enjoy the beauty? We begin a descent again, but this time, we have gained more wisdom from the last experience which will keep us from making the same mistakes and missteps as we travel toward the next mountain.

God knows that our lives with be filled with mountains to conquer. We cannot stay at the top or remain in the valleys. God continues to give us strength, knowledge and wisdom for these journeys. We know with certainty that God continues to travel with us to give us hope and faith. He will never leave us alone.

# -10-
# Stop Following the Wrong Crowd

Jerry was usually a loner. He did not have many friends at school or in the neighborhood where he lived. He spent most of his time studying and reading. His parents were always proud of his achievements at school. They were looking forward to his graduation from high school next year. He had planned to be an engineer when he graduated from college. One day, while he was at the store, he met a couple of boys, his age, who asked him if he wanted to hang out with them. He had seen them around, but did not know them. He wanted to have some friends, so he decided to tag along with them. They invited him to go to places where he really didn't feel comfortable, but he did not listen to his intuition which was telling him to go home. Each time he went with them, they told him they had some business to conduct, and he should wait outside.

On their third trip to the neighborhood, Jerry was waiting outside as usual. His new friends seemed to be taking longer than usual, and Jerry was beginning to get nervous. All of a sudden, he heard popping sounds. He began to run away, but some guys came running out into the street firing at his companions. One of the stray bullets hit Jerry in the back. He fell to the ground in pain. Everyone ran away and left him. He heard the sound of the police cars and realized that this was going to be trouble.

Jerry was taken to the hospital in serious condition. His parents rushed there to be by his side. Before they could speak to him, the police asked some questions. How did he know the boys involved, and why was he in that neighborhood? Jerry's parents were bewildered. They had no idea how or why he was there. They found out a serious crime had been committed, and Jerry had been identified as a look-out and therefore an accessory. They could not believe this was happening to their son. "He is a good boy. He has never Done anything wrong." The police seemed to be skeptical about their statements. Now, Jerry's future was in jeopardy, all because he chose to follow the wrong crowd.

How many times have we been in the wrong place at the wrong time because we chose to follow the wrong crowd? Sometimes we get caught in bad situations because of personal feelings of inadequacy. We don't want to be alone. We want to be popular. We want recognition. We allow our negative feelings to dictate to us even though we don't feel comfortable about what we are doing.

Before you get involved with any group of people, stop and think about a few things: 1. Why have these people approached me? 2. Are these the people I really want to be involved with? 3. Are they positive or negative people? 4. Do they have goals and beliefs that correspond with mine? 5. Do I feel uneasy or anxious whenever they are around?

If you have any doubts about a group or persons you are getting to know, take a step back and examine your feelings. If you are not comfortable, trust your intuition, and keep your distance until you have more information. It's better to be safe than sorry!

# -11-
# Do Something About It

Marie had fun with her family. She went shopping, to the movies and Sunday worship. She heard a very positive message, from the minister, about living life to the fullest. Everything was fine until Monday morning. As she rode the train, she began thinking about her co-workers, Alicia and Frank. She was sharing an office with these two people who constantly complain about everything, all day long.

Alicia was in a troubled relationship. She spent the day talking about all of the problems that her boyfriend constantly caused. As soon as Marie walked into the office, the complaints started with a familiar line - "Do you know what Myron did this weekend?" Alicia spent the day complaining about what Myron did and didn't do and how miserable she was in her relationship with him. He left on Friday and didn't return until Sunday night, or he spent her money, and she couldn't buy the food she needed for her children. He was always in trouble. When he was around, he verbally abused her and sometimes it became a physical altercation. She was always wondering what he would do next to make her angry. Alicia was frustrated with him.

Then there was Frank. He had been working for the company for several years but was always passed over for promotions. He blamed the management. He always said they didn't like him. They would never give him a chance to do anything different. He knew that he could do better work than some of the newer employees if they gave him a chance. He constantly criticized the management.

Marie listened to these complaints day in and day out. Most of the time she had a headache by the end of the day. It finally reached a point where she blurted out, "If you're not happy with your situations, why don't you do something about it?" They looked at her in disbelief. They didn't understand why she was so angry with them. She walked out of the office at lunch time and went to a nearby restaurant.

While she was sitting there, she began to realize a few things. Alicia, in her own way, was happy in her misery. It was the center of her life. If she didn't spend the day complaining about her boyfriend, she wouldn't have anything of substance to talk about. Frank could have received promotions if he had gone back to school and earned an advanced degree, but he didn't feel like putting in the effort. He was lazy.

Marie finally understood that she should do something about her own situation. She went to her supervisor and requested a change in her work assignment. When her supervisor realized she had management skills, she was given some options to move into other departments, and the one that she chose gave her a higher salary and better benefits. She now had her own office and an assistant who worked for her. She was very happy with her new position, and she was also happy to be away from her former, complaining co-workers. And what happened to Alicia and Frank? A new worker was assigned to their office, and they began unloading their complaints on her! They chose not to do anything about their situations. If you are stuck in a situation, remember that nothing will change until you decide to do something about it.

## -12-
## Don't Mix Business with Pleasure

Marcie was a loner. She never had very many friends. She spent most of her time concentrating on her career. Her skills had helped her to find the perfect job with opportunities for advancement. There were several employees in her department, and they seemed to be very friendly. Marcie began to make friends with several of them. When they asked her to join them for social occasions, she was happy to be included.

Marcie was happy to have friends to confide in. One co-worker, in particular, used to talk to Marcie about her previous jobs and relationships. Marcie discussed many things about her life including problems that she had to overcome. The co-worker seemed to be very supportive and always had advice for Marcie.

One day, Marcie told her that she was being considered for a promotion. The co-worker was not very happy to hear that news. She had worked for the company much longer than Marcie and had never been approached about a raise or promotion. Her attitude toward Marcie changed, but she managed to hide her anger and jealousy. On a day that Marcie went to another branch for a meeting, the co-worker saw an opportunity to sabotage Marcie's chances for the promotion. She told her supervising manager personal things about Marcie's life, and she exaggerated the situations to make them seem worse than they actually were. This caused the manager to reconsider Marcie for the new position. Marcie did not receive the promotion, but a few weeks later, she found out the co-worker had applied for the same position.

Marcie learned a valuable lesson when the manager spoke to her and recounted the information that had been supplied by the co-worker. Marcie was very disappointed. She thought she had friends on the job, but now, she realized that she had been taken advantage of. She remembered a quote: "Don't mix business with pleasure."

Carolyn was very attracted to the manager on her job. He was always flirting with her, and she was flattered. She finally consented to a date. He was a charming guy, and before she knew it, they were having an affair. She did not realize that he flirted with other women as well. One evening, he told her that he was working late. She decided to go out with the girls to a favorite restaurant. When she walked in, who did she see – her manager/lover with another woman. She was furious and very hurt. The next day, she confronted him and broke off the relationship. He wasn't pleased and decided to make her life miserable on the job. He complained about everything that she did and humiliated her in front of her co-workers. After a few weeks, she was forced to resign. This type of scenario also happens to men who have women as supervisors and managers. The Lesson: "Don't mix business with pleasure."

Many times, people are happy to have the social interaction of the job. If they don't meet lots of people in other places, the job seems like the perfect opportunity to develop friends and find relationships. While things are going well, it seems like the perfect dream situation, but when things go wrong, as they often do, it becomes the perfect nightmare. Don't make the mistake of putting your job and career in jeopardy because you have not exercised wisdom and common sense. People on the job are people on the job. They may be friendly, but they should not be included in your close circle of friends. They should not have access to your personal life. If they become jealous of your success, they will turn on you and work to destroy all that you have accomplished. They will tell and gossip about the details of your personal life, and you will be left to wonder why people are treating you differently. Remember, "Don't mix business with pleasure."

# -13-
# Stop Wasting Energy

I was shopping at a local appliance store recently and listened to a conversation between a son and his elderly mother as they shopped for new appliances. The son was trying to explain to her that she needed new equipment to replace the old, outdated ones that she had in her home for more than 20 years. He went on to explain that the old items used up too much energy and caused her to spend more than necessary on her utility bill. The new equipment would save her considerable money by running more efficiently and using less energy. It was a difficult sell, but he finally convinced her to let go of those energy-draining appliances.

As humans, we also allow situations in our lives to consume too much of our energy. Old hurts and disappointments drain us every time we revisit them, and yet we don't want to give them up. We don't want to try a new way of living or a new way to make use of our energy.

I received a series of emails from my Life Coach with a question. I, in turn, decided to come up with some similar questions for my Toastmasters' Club and asked them to think about them during the next few days. I am asking you the same questions:

What if you had 30 days left on earth? What would your feelings be? Who would you want to spend those 30 days with? What would matter, and what would suddenly become trivial to you? What activities would you pursue, and which ones would you abandon? Would you spend those 30 days living as a victim, or would you make a bucket list of things to pursue and get busy?

If you could imagine yourself in this circumstance, I think you would begin to realize that you have been wasting energy on things, people and situations that are not really important to your life's purpose. Some people have not really thought about their purpose and what their passion is because they continue to waste energy on negative situations and people.

The cost of wasting your energy can be prohibitive. Your health can be negatively affected from the constant drain on your energy. You may begin to experience frequent headaches and neck pain. The drain can lower your resistance and make you vulnerable to serious illness. The friends, who are really special, leave your life because they are looking for something and someone who is positive to relate to. Their patience runs out as you continue to focus on negative people. You make careless and costly mistakes because you are too caught up in the drama of those energy-draining people and situations.

How many opportunities have you missed because you think you have all the time in the world? How many times have you pushed away the person who really loves you because you think you have time to make that commitment? How many times have you put off your vacation by convincing yourself that you can go next year? When will you stop wasting your energy on the negative side of life and start investing in the things and people who will bring you joy?

If you had 30 days, I hope that you would do the best things each day that will give you the most benefit in living your purpose and passion.

## -14-
## It's Okay to Fall

Alan's four year old son, Brandon, wanted to learn how to ride his bicycle without the training wheels he had been dependant on for several weeks. Brandon was sure that he was ready, but each day was a challenge. After a few minutes of riding, he would fall. Sometimes he was uninjured, but several times he scraped his knees and elbows. His father wanted to put the training wheels back, but Brandon wanted to keep trying. Alan was afraid that his son would get hurt, but Brandon would not give up. Finally, one day, he started to ride and did not fall. He went to the corner and around the block without one incident. Alan was proud of his son for having a determination that would not allow him to stop trying until he succeeded.

Alan learned a valuable lesson from his four year old son. He always wanted to have his own business, but when he started, there were many obstacles. Each time he faced a setback, he became more discouraged. He failed many times and finally decided that he would give up on his dream. While he was packing up his equipment, he thought about how his son was so determined to learn how to ride his bicycle. He remembered how many days Brandon went back outside and got on his bicycle and tried again until he finally began to ride without falling. Alan decided to unpack his equipment and try again. He called a prospective customer who had been uncertain about giving Alan a contract. The customer was happy to hear from him. He said that his previous contractor had disappointed him, and he had been looking for Alan's business card. He made an appointment to see him, and gave him a contract for all of his work. The new customer referred other customers to Alan. His business suddenly began to pick up, and he had to hire additional help to keep up with the new contracts coming in.

In life, we will fail many times before we finally succeed. We have to remember a few things. First, we cannot be afraid to fail. Failing doesn't mean that you will not succeed. Every failure teaches a lesson. You learn from your mistakes. Second, you have to stay focused on your ultimate goal. Third, don't allow anything to destroy your confidence. Fourth, do something everyday, even if it's something small. Some days you will accomplish more, but some days you will accomplish less. That's okay. As long as you commit to trying each day, you are getting closer to success.

Finally, prepare and keep a written plan or a blueprint to follow. During the days when things are not going the way you want, review your plan. You may need to make some alterations, but the basic plan is still the map to follow to your ultimate success.

Failure is part of success. If you read stories about those who have been successful, you will see they failed many times before they succeeded, but they did not give up because the failures were only temporary. This applies to business, education and life. The road to success will have potholes, detours and a few other rough spots. You may fall into the potholes, get temporarily lost on the detours and stumble on the rough spots, but you must keep going in order to reach your destination.

## -15-
## Someday Never Comes

When Diana Ross decided to leave the Supremes, she sang the song, *"Someday, We'll be Together."* We all knew that someday would never come again for that dynamic group of ladies. We even remember that phrase in fairytales: *"Someday, my prince will come."* How long have we been waiting for that dream to come true?

How many of us use the term "someday" when we are asked about a goal that we are planning to pursue? *Someday, I will be successful. Someday, I will get this done. Someday, I will have the money that I need. Someday, I will find my one true love.* As long as we engage in the fantasy of someday, nothing will get done. How long are you willing to indulge in this fantasy? When will you decide that "today" is the day to take action to reach your "someday?"

Your reality is in today. This is the day to make the most of every opportunity. This is the day to sit down with your finances and set a budget that is realistic. This is the day to start getting rid of the clutter in your home. This is the day to do more social networking if you want to meet new people. Today is the day to begin working on a new business opportunity or project that will help to build your financial security. Today is the day to begin a new eating plan or health and exercise plan.

We know in our hearts and minds that tomorrow is not promised to us. The longer we put off doing the things that we want to do and procrastinating about goals and projects, the greater the chance that we will never accomplish anything.

If we keep waiting for someday, we will come to a time when we say, *I wish I had.*

## -16-
## Missed Opportunities

Marilyn always wanted to own her own business. She could imagine what it would be like if she took a leap of faith in order to make a start. Over the years, several opportunities presented themselves. Each time, Marilyn failed to make the connection. She was unsure of her abilities. She was afraid of failure. She thought she had time to make up her mind. Each time she finally summoned up the courage to become involved, the opportunity had passed her by. She convinced herself that she would not let the next opportunity get away from her, but when someone approached her about a partnership, she failed to act because of the negative thoughts swimming around in her mind. Those negative thoughts have defeated her desire every time.

How many times have you let the perfect opportunity pass you by? God does not send one opportunity for you. He sends many. Each opportunity comes with blessings and curses.

When I was a little girl, my parents wanted to buy a house. They would go on house tours in different areas of New York and New Jersey. They even worked with a realtor. I used to get excited about each of the houses toured. I kept thinking, "This is going to be the one." But the days, months and years went buy, and they missed out on the opportunity to buy. In the later years of their lives, they always wondered what would have happened if they had bought one of those houses.

Successful people are risk takers. They know it is important to step out of their comfort zones to do something new and different if they want to realize their dreams.

Joe thought he had met the woman of his dreams. She was sweet and kind and seemed to share all of his interests. Sharon wanted to talk about marriage, but Joe was afraid to make a commitment. They had been dating for a few months when Sharon told him she had to visit her relatives in another state. She had taken short weekend trips before, but this time, she said she would be gone for a month. Joe wanted to go with her, but she said he would be bored. While she was gone, he tried to call her but kept getting her voice mail. The one time she called, she could not talk long. She was in a hurry.

One day, Joe's friend, Harold told him he saw a posting on Facebook featuring Sharon with another man and the caption read, "Congratulations on your marriage!" Joe couldn't believe it. How could she do that to him? His dream girl had turned into a nightmare. Joe told his friends that he would never trust another woman!

Some people miss out on the perfect relationship because they are afraid of being hurt. Someone broke their hearts, and now they think the same thing will happen again and again. To them, it is not worth the risk.

## -17-
## Calm Down

Shannon left her home a few minutes late, and the bus was also delayed causing her to arrive at work at 9:30 instead of 9:00 AM. After her boss reprimanded her, she went to her cubicle. As she began to organize her work for the day, she noticed her stapler was missing. She searched her desk and the drawers but could not find it. She noticed a stapler on her co-worker's desk that looked just like hers. She stormed over and accused the worker of stealing it. The worker tried to tell her that she did not take her stapler, but Shannon was not hearing it. She began a loud argument with the worker which resulted in a shoving match. Her boss came out and immediately called Shannon into his office. She was so angry that she also shouted obscenities at her boss which resulted in her immediate suspension without pay. Shannon could not return to work for two weeks. After she went home, Shannon remembered that she had loaned her stapler to another co-worker who was not at work that day. Her anger had cost her a friendship and two weeks' pay. She was now worried that this incident could also result in her termination from the job.

Anger is a destructive force. Once you allow anger to take control of your emotions, it will continue to escalate. It can cause you to say and do things that you would not ordinarily do. It can lead to hurt feelings, and, in extreme cases, violence. Words spoken in anger cannot be erased. It can destroy relationships, friendships and even cost you a job.

We all experience feelings of anger, but there are a few things we can do to regain control before destructive things happen.

1.  Before you speak to anyone, calm down. You can do that by going for a walk, taking deep breaths and/or counting backward from 10 to 1, or 100 to 1 if the angry feelings are overwhelming. Listen to some music, or watch something funny. Diversions will help you to get your emotions under control.

2.  Before you speak to the person, speak to someone else and explain your feelings. A brief discussion with someone else can help to diffuse your anger. Another person may be able to offer some helpful suggestions. Make sure the person you choose is a positive, calm person who will not add fuel to your anger.

3.  Think and consider that there may be something else at the root of your anger. You might be lashing out at someone because you are upset about a totally unrelated matter. Someone may have hurt your feelings earlier, or you may have received some bad news. Anger is often a reaction to another troubling situation. Shannon had received some bad news before she left the house that morning which caused her to be late. If she had discussed her situation with a friend before she arrived at work, she may have been able to calm down.

4.  Think about the physical and emotional effects of your anger. Angry people, 9 out of 10 times, develop high blood pressure and other health problems. Angry people are often isolated people because no one wants to be around them. The after effects can be guilt, shame

and depression over the way you spoke and behaved in front of other people.

Don't allow anger to control you. Negative emotions unleashed always result in negative outcomes.

# -18-
# Give Your Brain a Break

When I joined an exercise program, the instructor told us that it was important to take a one day break between intensive exercise sessions in order to give our muscles a chance to recover from the strain. That one day break would allow the muscles to relax and be ready for the next session.

Our brains and emotions need the same type of attention. There are times that we experience a very emotionally charged situation that lasts for a prolonged period of time. It may also be a health problem that we are working to overcome, the passing of a loved one or a difficult job task that requires our concentration day in and day out until completion. In the aftermath of the situation, we think that we can move on to the next set of situations without really giving ourselves a chance to release and regroup. The result can be an emotional burnout.

We need recovery time. We need some down time. We need to allow the pressure to subside. We need time to refocus. We need to allow ourselves time to heal. Take time to relax and have some fun. Your brain will thank you.

## -19-
## Who Knows Your Story?

When people attend funerals, they are often amazed when they hear the obituary of the deceased because there are so many things that people were not aware of concerning the person's life. It makes you wish that you had taken the time to learn more about them during their lifetime.

During your life, you will experience many phases and journeys. Each journey involves a set of friends and contacts who will be familiar with that part of your life, but then you move on to the another phase. You may move to another part of the country. You may have several career changes; you might have awards given at special events; you may have special talents that you have not revealed to your current friends. If you are fortunate, there may be people who are in your life through many of your journeys, but sometimes, people, who know the most, die before you.

There is one thing, you can do now, to make sure that your full story is known: prepare your biography. You don't have to be an eloquent writer. You don't have to be able to write the great American novel. Keep a journal that highlights the events of your life. Write about all of the things that have been important to you over the years and the legacy that you want to leave. Keep the journal or document with your important papers. Give a copy to the person who is closest to you. Make sure that someone knows your story.

# -20-
# Intervention

Carolyn and Jacob's marriage was on the rocks. The divorce was complicated and very unpleasant. Each of them wanted control of the house and most of the possessions. Each time they met with the attorneys, it ended with bitter words and no resolution. Both Carolyn and Jacob decided that neither would move out of the house. Carolyn lived upstairs, and Jacob lived downstairs. It was a constant battle with emotional outbursts daily.

Everyone became involved in the battle. Friends and family were taking sides. The children were torn between the two parents. Their jobs suffered from the fall out. They could not have any social connections. Life was becoming impossible.

One evening, there was a terrible storm with hurricane force winds. Neither Carolyn nor Jacob could get home before the storm started. They each had to stay near their jobs until the storm subsided. When they arrived home, they were shocked to see the condition of the house. The high winds caused a huge tree to fall on the house, and the electrical wires sparked causing a fire. The house was destroyed. Carolyn and Jacob were devastated. Everything was gone.

The insurance company paid for the house and the contents. The check was in the names of Carolyn and Jacob. They split the proceeds. There was nothing left to fight over. They had to find new places to live.

Devine intervention solved their problem since they were not civil enough to work things out. Sometimes God steps in to provide the solution. It may not be the solution you expect or want, but the problem will be resolved when God makes a move.

## -21-
## Don't Live With Agitation

Jan and Carl have been together for several years. They are very close, but sometimes Carl will do something that really aggravates her. Jan loves him, so she doesn't want to start an argument by telling Carl what he has done to offend her. As time goes by, Jan becomes more agitated by Carl's lack of sensitivity to her feelings. Instead of talking to him about the situation, she holds her tongue and her anger, but those feelings have to come out. She begins to take her frustration out on her friends and co-workers. She becomes more and more unhappy about her life because she expects Carl to know how she is feeling. She begins to treat him with contempt whenever he says something to her that she does not like. Her agitation has turned her into an unpleasant person.

If someone interferes with your peace, you have an obligation to yourself to tell them what has hurt you. Trying to hold it in or make do with the situation will only cause increasing feelings of anger and resentment. Sometimes people are not aware that they have said or done something to offend you. It is up to you to sit down with them and explain your feelings at the moment of the occurrence. You should have emotional boundaries, and it is important to let people know when they cross the line. You cannot spare someone's feelings at the expense of your own. Seek to be understood while you also seek to understand through meaningful conversations.

**-22-**
# The End is Also the Beginning

Traci had been involved with her high school sweetheart, Jim, for more than 10 years. They did everything together in high school. The went to the same college, and then they got married as soon as they graduated and began their careers. Traci always said that Jim was the love of her life, and she could not imagine life without him. They had their usual share of disagreements, but they appeared to be able to resolve their differences, or so Traci thought.

Jim had to take a business trip. While he was away, he met with several national executives for his company. That's when he met Amanda. For them, it was love at first sight. Amanda and Jim had a lot in common and spent many hours talking about their dreams and goals. When Jim returned home, he could not stop thinking about Amanda. She was very special to him, but he also still had feelings for Traci. Their relationship continued to erode as their disagreements became more intense. Sometimes Jim did not come home. Traci was distressed. This was the only man she had ever been in love with.

Finally, the moment of truth came for Jim and Traci. They sat down and had a long talk. They both admitted that their feelings for each other had changed. They wanted out of the marriage, but had been afraid to take the steps toward ending a relationship they thought would last forever.

After the divorce, they both felt lost. They had to begin thinking for one instead of two. After a few months, Jim went on another business trip. While he was having dinner, he spotted Amanda. They had not spoken to each other for a long time. He invited her to join him for dinner. Suddenly, he did not feel alone. Could this be the beginning of something wonderful for him?

Traci decided to move to another town. She joined a social club because she wanted to meet some new people. She had been lonely and felt isolated in her former home because everyone knew her as part of a couple. They did not call her after she and Jim were divorced. She met a few people, but she still felt lonely. At one of the gatherings, one of the women invited her to come to a dinner dance. She wanted Traci to meet her brother, Tom. Traci was hesitant to accept at first, but then she agreed to come. When she met Tom, she was pleasantly surprised by his kindness and sense of humor. She found herself talking to him for hours. They made a date for the movies. Traci was encouraged. She was finally beginning to feel that life was worth living again.

Sometimes, we think that a devastating loss is the end of the world. We can't imagine how we can go on. We don't even want to try. We isolate ourselves because we don't think people will understand. It is important to remember that God always has a new beginning for us, and sometimes, in order for God to bring something new, we have to let something else end. You may have to take a detour, but it is not the end of the road. It is the beginning of a new journey.

Remember the words in Isaiah 43:18 -19 "Forget the former things; do not dwell on the past. See, I am doing a new thing...I am making a way in the desert and streams in the wasteland."

# -23-
# Get Your Affairs in Order

Years ago, my mother had a friend who lost her husband of 50 years. They were completely devoted to each other. Her husband always took care of her. She did not have to work. He had a good job and retired with a pension and substantial savings which enabled them to have a comfortable life together. Not long after his retirement, he suddenly died. Mrs. Moore was devastated. It had always been just the two of them, and he had always taken care of everything. After the funeral, she realized that she did not know anything about the bills, how to take care of the house or manage her financial affairs. She did not know where to find any of his important documents. She was completely bewildered. She had never written a check or paid a bill. She didn't know if the house was mortgaged or free and clear.

Eventually, she had to hire someone to manage the finances and help her make decisions. She became a total recluse. She had withdrawn from her friends and family and lived the balance of her life alone.

There are too many of us living day to day without having our affairs in order. We would like to live forever, but the reality is we won't. There are several things we can do to make reasonably certain that our wishes are followed.

1. Prepare a Healthcare Proxy. If you become too ill to make decisions for yourself, a designated person will be

able to manage your health care needs and treatments. That person will be empowered to carry out your wishes.

2.  Prepare a Last Will and Testament and keep it up to date. Designate an Executor or Executrix (man or woman) and an alternate if that person cannot serve. If your desires change, be sure to have a new Will prepared as soon as possible and destroy the old copy. You can keep the original with your attorney or in a secure place in your home. Do not put it in a safe deposit box. The bank will not grant access without legal process after you die.

3.  Keep a list of your assets and other important documents, like insurance policies and investments, in a safe place. Also keep a list of those who should be contacted in the event of illness or death. Prepare an updated biography and a list of instructions to be followed.

4.  Be sure to designate a beneficiary for each of your insurance policies, bank accounts and annuities.

5.  Have one person, whom you absolutely trust, to have knowledge of everything. It has to be someone who will keep your confidentiality. If you don't want to give that information to one person, then give the documents or copies to your attorney who will then work with your executor to make sure all legal matters are handled properly after your death.

6.  Be sure to have an attorney who is experienced with Wills, Estates and Trusts. They will review and give you advice on the best procedures to follow.

Do not assume family will make the right decisions for everyone or get along with each other. Many families split when there are questions about who has the right to assets and custody of minor children. None of us wants to think about end of life issues, but it is important to get our affairs in order.

## -24-
## You are Not Alone

It was a stormy night. Jah-ella left school later than usual. As she drove toward the highway, she saw warning signs posted redirecting traffic because of an accident that had closed several lanes. The traffic was very congested. She wasn't sure of the direction to take, but she thought she remembered an alternate route that would take her around the accident site.

The road was not well lit, and there were no cars. She thought this was the perfect way to go. As she proceeded, she was sure that she was taking the best route. Suddenly, she found herself in deep water. Because the road was dark, she could not tell how deep the water was, so she tried to drive through to the other side. It was not a good judgment call. The water came up over the wheels and began to seep into the car. The car stalled and Jah-ella was now stuck in deep water. "Why did I choose this unknown path instead of staying on the main road with other people who could provide help if I got stuck?"

She could not open the car doors because of the water pressure. There was no way out, and she could not find her phone to call for help. With no options or help on the horizon, Jah-ella began to cry. She thought about her family. What if she never saw them again? She started seeing images of her life flashing before her eyes. She closed her eyes and began to pray. She told God how much she loved her family and wanted to see them again. She asked God to forgive her for all of her mistakes. All she wanted was another chance.

As she kept praying for a miracle, she suddenly felt the car moving. She began to scream because she thought the car was being swept away deeper into the water, and she would drown. When she opened her eyes, she realized there were bright lights behind her coming from a very large truck. The driver had hooked a chain to her bumper and began to pull her car back out of the water. After she was safe, she asked the truck driver how he found her. He told her that someone always get stuck when they take this abandoned road in a rain storm. They think it's a better way to go, so he always comes to look just in case someone is trapped. He didn't want anyone to be left alone and in distress.

The truck driver pulled her car to a safe place and then drove her home. She was so happy to see her mother that she hugged her and held on tight. She told her that she thought she was going to die without seeing her again.

There are times that we go off in directions that do not follow the path that God has directed us to take. We think that we know a better way or a shortcut to what we want, but then we end up in deep waters of trouble and despair. It seems that no one is around to help us. If we stop and pray and ask God to help us and redirect our lives, He will respond. We can always depend on God. He will not leave us alone in our struggles, even when we have not obeyed his word. If we call out to Him, he will find us and bring us back. Just when you think all hope is lost, God reaches out with his saving power to bring us out of the waters of hopelessness and despair. You are not alone.

"I will search for the lost and bring back the strays. I will bind up the injured and strengthen the weak." (Ezekiel 34:16)

Do you remember a time that you felt lost and alone because you strayed away from God?

## -25-
## The Teen Scene - Overcoming Procrastination

Jamal finished dinner and cleared the table. He had a Math exam scheduled for the next day, but he still had time to study, or so he thought. Before his mother could ask him any questions, he was planted in front of the television playing a video game. After all, it was still early. His mother asked him if he was prepared for the test. He said, "Of course. I've got it covered." He continued playing the game.

Finally, his mother insisted that he go to his room to study. He turned off the game and went upstairs to his room, but then his cell phone rang. One of his friends called to ask him about the exam. Since he could not answer the question, he told his friend that he was studying and had to get off the phone. After he hung up, he remembered that he had promised to call a couple of other friends. "I have time. It's still early." He called his friends, but they were studying and could not talk. Jamal made several more calls before it finally dawned on him that it was getting late, and he was getting sleepy. He opened his textbook and looked at his notes. Suddenly, he wasn't very confident about taking the test. He tried to study, but he was too sleepy to concentrate. "Why didn't I begin to study at the beginning of the week?" He could not decipher the lesson in only one night.

Now, he tried to think up excuses to avoid taking the test. Maybe he could pretend to be sick, or maybe he could tell the teacher that he had to go to the hospital with the family to see someone, and he forgot to take his Math book. If he took the test and failed, how would he explain it to his Mom? He was too sleepy to think of any more excuses. As he was falling asleep, he kept thinking, "Why didn't I study when I was supposed to? If I fail, I'll be in a lot of trouble."

The alarm clock sounded, and Jamal jumped up in a state of panic. He rushed to take a shower and get dressed. He ran downstairs to make breakfast. Just then, his mother called out to him. "Jamal, what are you doing up so early? It's Saturday morning." He suddenly realized that he had been dreaming the whole time about taking his Math exam! He ate his breakfast and went upstairs to get his Math book. "I'm not going to turn my nightmare into reality. I'm going to stop procrastinating!" Jamal set up a study schedule which he would follow for the rest of the semester. He did not want to feel that degree of panic again. He realized that procrastination is the enemy of success. He pasted a sign on his bedroom wall that said, "Do It Now!" He was thankful that God had given him a glimpse of a potential reality in his dream.

There are several ways to overcome the habit of procrastination:

1. At the beginning of the week, make a list of all tasks and assignments to be completed.

2. Put a date for completion next to each item.

3. Begin working on Monday.

4. Do the assignments for the day before you take a break.

5. Cut down on television and video games. They waste time.

6. Develop a "do it now" attitude.

7. Review your list to be sure you did not skip anything.

By the end of the week, you will be happy with your accomplishments, and then you can relax and have fun.

# -26-
## The Teen Scene - Making Choices

Jamal and his friends were entering their senior year of high school last year. All of them had plans to go on to college. They knew the value of a higher education. Planning is essential, so they set appointments to meet with the college guidance counselor, all of them except Chris. He always had other things to do. He told his friends that he already knew what to do, and he did not need to sit and listen to a counselor.

The group met with the counselor without Chris. They received valuable information that they shared with their parents. The counselor also told them about coaching classes for the S.A.T. exam. They signed up for the sessions, and again, they asked Chris to attend. They waited for him, but Chris was a no show. He told them later that he was too busy. Jamal and his friends decided they would not try to persuade him anymore.

As the year progressed, the group of friends had study sessions together and worked on the practice exams while Chris studied occasionally on his own. The day for the S.A.T. came. The group was ready. Chris was not. While they were taking the exam, Chris tried to copy answers from another student. The exam proctor saw something suspicious and began to watch Chris. He was caught and not allowed to take another exam. In addition, he was not allowed to graduate.

Chris was in a real jam. He could not apply for college. He would not be able to attend in the Fall with his friends, and now, he had to tell his parents. When he ran into Jamal, he said, "I wish I had listened to you and the other guys. I made the wrong choice, and now I'm in hot water with my parents."

Making good choices will make you feel better about yourself and your life. There are several ways to make good choices. Carefully consider all of the options. Help yourself by getting all of the information in order to make an informed choice. Ignore the bad ideas that might pop into your head. Think about what will happen if you make the wrong choice. Discuss your options with your parents, and once you decide, make a plan and follow through. Being able to make good choices, shows that you are growing in your sense of responsibility.

## -27-
## Love Makes Your World Go Round

*Love* is a universally recognized word.  Ministers preach about it; choirs sing about it; R & B groups declare it, and poets rhyme about it.  There are many writings about love, but the best can be found in the Bible, specifically 1 Corinthians 13:1-13.  This particular chapter is devoted to the principles of true Christian love:

"Love is patient; love is kind.  It does not envy; it does not boast; it is not proud.  It is not rude; it is not self-seeking. It is not easily angered; it keeps no record of wrongs. Love does not delight in evil but rejoices in the truth.  It always protects, always trusts, always hopes, always perseveres.  Love never fails."  (1 Corinthians 13:4-8a)

If we could remember these principles and apply them in our daily lives, we would have more peace.  The Bible tells us that we will not truly know the peace of God if we don't walk in the path of unconditional love.  God knows that we are a work in progress, and we will not abide by 1 Corinthians, chapter 13 everyday or in every situation.  That does not stop God from loving us unconditionally.  He loves us when we have doubts and fears. He loves us when we fail to acknowledge Him in every situation.  He continues to love us through our mistakes and missteps. He even loves us when we don't think we deserve His love.

We will know the joy of true peace when we learn to operate in Christian love.  When life's trials threaten to diminish your decision to walk in love, read 1 Corinthians 13. Remember that God loves you, and His love never fails.

Find a scripture about love and read it every day until it becomes a part of you. Also, keep this prayer from God with you this week:

"My child, the fruit of My Spirit is patience, love, peace, joy and faithfulness. If you focus on these things, you will have peace. As you walk in love, I will clear the path for you. I will remove the obstacles and bring you the blessings. Trust and lean on me." – Almighty God

# Section Three - Bible Study Devotions

## -1-
## Mind Your Own Business

It was Sunday morning, and Sherrell was rushing around the house gathering her belongings so she could get to church on time. In fact, she wanted to be early because she was sure that she would be able to gather some juicy gossip as people came in.

She walked through the lobby as if she wasn't paying attention, but her ears were alert for some news. She overheard one lady, named Marion, talking about an affair she attended at Antun's. It was a fashion show, and she planned to buy some new clothes for her trip. This wasn't the juiciest gossip, but Sherrell could add that news to any other items she gathered that day.

When she arrived home, Sherrell had dinner and then proceeded to make her calls. Of course, as news spread from one person to the next, information was added and deleted to make the story more appealing. The gossip made full circle back to the church.

On the following Sunday, when Sherrell returned to church, she noticed people whispering. Some of them seemed to be very distressed. As she got closer, she overheard some of what was being discussed. Someone was saying they had just heard that Marion was having an affair with Jean's husband, whose name is Anton, and she was buying new clothes because they were taking a trip together! What was even worse, they were blaming Sherrell for telling everyone about it. She couldn't believe what she was hearing. Now she was the subject of the gossip.

Sherrell's gossip had been twisted. She was embarrassed. The church people began to shun Anton because they thought he was despicable. His wife left him because she didn't believe him. Marion was being snubbed because they thought she was a hussy, among other things. And no one was talking to Sherrell.

Gossip can cause hurt and humiliation. It can hurt innocent bystanders and destroy lives, especially when it gets out of control. The best solution for gossip is to mind your own business.

The Bible says, "The tongue has the power of life and death, and those who love it will eat its fruit." (Proverbs 18:21)

"If anyone considers himself/herself religious and yet does not keep a tight rein on the tongue, they deceive themselves and their religion is worthless." (James 1:26)

Do you know someone like Sherrell? Could it be you?

## -2-
## Ripples of Change

When you sit by a lake, you are mesmerized by its calm, soothing qualities. The water has the look of a smooth piece of glass. What happens when you decide to throw a stone into the water? The stone becomes the center of an increasing circle of ripples that spreads out and disrupts the stillness of the water. The water begins to shift in several areas, and even spreads to the shoreline. All of the water, around the stone, is disturbed and forced to shift to a new position. Just one small stone, thrown into the water, changes everything. Eventually, the water settles in its new spot resulting in a different shape.

Change, in our lives, creates the same ripple effect. We may do only one thing. It could be changing or leaving a job, moving, losing weight or beginning a new relationship. We look at these changes and believe they will not have a significant effect on the other areas of our lives, but we soon realize this one change has shifted everything that was normal to us. We begin to feel uneasy and uncomfortable because we want the change, but we also want everything else to remain the same. We don't want to lose the things that are familiar and comfortable.

When a shift occurs in our lives, it forces us to look at all areas and accept that things will be different than they were before, even after everything settles. We have to realize the ripple effect will shift the way we relate to people and the way they relate to us. The ripple may force some people out of our lives, but it may also bring new people in. The change even forces us to look at ourselves differently. The ripple will force us to experience new places and situations. It will bring changes in habits and other behaviors. If we fight against the changes, that are inevitable, we will feel confused, anxious and miserable because we keep trying to hold onto what was. If we accept the changes, we look forward, with anticipation, to the new things that will begin to come in and reshape our lives.

We periodically need ripples of change. Don't be afraid to throw a stone into the water. Look forward to watching the ripples and the new formations that will result. Keep an open mind, even if the stone seems to create a negative splash. Something new and wonderful is waiting to flow, through the ripples, into your life. Throw a stone into your lake, and embrace the change.

Scripture for meditation:

"Forget the former things; do not dwell on the past. See, I am doing a new thing! Now it springs up; do you not perceive it? I am making a way in the desert and streams in the wasteland." (Isaiah 43:18-19)

Has a stone been thrown into your life? How has the ripple effect changed you? Are you fighting against it or accepting it?

**-3-**
# The Essence of Your Faith

When trials and troubles challenge you, when life seems to have too many mountains to climb or valleys to cross, your faith can take a beating, but there is one thing at the heart of your faith that will keep you going if you use it – Prayer.

Prayer is your foundation. The more you pray, the stronger your faith becomes. The more you pray, the stronger your confidence becomes. Prayer will build and reinforce your faith when the world tries to tear you down. Prayer gives you something that the world cannot take away from you. It gives you peace.

Prayer brings protection in the storm. It activates God's blessing power. Begin your day with prayer. Pray at midday and in the evening. Pray when you are sad and when you are happy. Pray in the good times and the bad times. Pray until you have a breakthrough, and then say prayers of thanksgiving to God.

The Bible speaks about the times you should pray:

"Be joyful always; pray continually; give thanks in all circumstances, for this is God's will for you." (1 Thessalonians 5:16-17)

"Do not be anxious about anything, but in everything, by prayer and petition, present your requests to God, and the peace of God, which transcends all understanding, will guard your hearts and your minds..." (Philippians 4:6-7)

"Love your enemies and pray for those who persecute you." (Matthew 5:44)

"...Pray for those who mistreat you." (Luke 6:28)

"Pray that you will not fall into temptation." (Luke 22:40)

"We do not know what we ought to pray for, but the Spirit himself intercedes for us with groans that words cannot express." (Romans 8:26)

"Is any one of you in trouble? He or she should pray." (James 5:13a)

"The prayer of a righteous person is powerful and effective." (James 5:16b)

Answered prayer is one of the best gifts that we receive from God. May the peace of God and the fresh anointing of the Holy Spirit rest in your thoughts, rule in your dreams today and conquer all of your fears about tomorrow. May God manifest himself in ways that you have never imagined and move you away from those things that are harmful to your spirit as He brings you closer to the victories that you seek. Amen.

Did you take time to pray today?

## -4-
## Believe and Achieve

We settle for mediocrity and dissatisfaction because we believe this is our lot in life. We stay in the same dead-end job because we don't trust in our ability to secure a new position. We accept relationships and friendships that are toxic because we are afraid of being alone.

Whenever we think about trying something new, we defeat ourselves before we get started. As soon as we say, "I don't think I can do this," or "I don't know if I can succeed," we are doomed. When we speak words of defeat before we begin, or while we are in the midst of trying to accomplish something, we are committing ourselves to take the path that leads to failure.

What you believe and speak will turn on the positive or negative forces inside you. In Genesis 1, verse 3, God said, "Let there be light," and there was light." He didn't start out by saying, "I wonder if I can do this?" or "What if this doesn't work?"

God has already put the power within us to have our heart's desires. We have to turn it on by speaking positive words. "I believe I can; I will, and I won't give up until I achieve." You may want to have your own business. You may want to go back to school or find a new job. You may want to be an athlete, writer, singer or dancer. If you believe in yourself and the power that God has placed in you, and if you pray and speak positive affirmations everyday and night, God will make a way for you to achieve what you believe. It may not happen today or even tomorrow, but God will not fail to bring the blessings. Trust God to make a way even when you don't see the possibilities. Believe that you will achieve. Believe that you will succeed. Believe in yourself and have faith in God. His love never fails.

Strengthen your belief with these scriptures everyday this week:

"I know the plans I have for you," declares the Lord, "plans to prosper you and not to harm you, plans to give you hope and a future." (Jeremiah 29:11)

"Stay at peace with God. In this way, prosperity will come to you. Accept instruction from him and keep his words in your heart. Then, when you pray, you will hear from him, and he fulfill your desires. What you decide on will be done and light will shine on your way." (Portions of Job 22:21-28)

"If you believe, you will receive whatever you ask for in prayer." (Matthew 21:22)

"Nothing is impossible with God." (Luke 1:37)

"Ask and it will be given to you; seek and you will find; knock and the door will be opened to you." (Matthew 7:7)

"Then Jesus said...Go! It will be done as you believed it would." (Matthew 8:13)

"Ask and you will receive, and your joy will be complete." (John 16:24b)

"Delight yourself in the Lord and he will give you the desires of your heart." (Psalm 37:4)

"In all your ways acknowledge him, and he will make your paths straight." (Proverbs 3:6)

"Stop doubting and believe." (John 20:27c)

What do you believe you can achieve? Are you moving forward to achieve what you believe?

## -5-
## Be True to Yourself

In the course of a day, you are pushed and pulled in many different directions by friends, family and co-workers who have agendas which, many times, are not in your best interests. They may be happy with what they have forced you to do, but you are left feeling uncomfortable, nervous and anxious about the decisions you have made and actions you have taken. In your heart and spirit, you know these paths are not the ones you want to follow, and yet you feel pressured to please others. You are not doing what God wants you to do.

Jeremiah 29:11 says, "I know the plans I have for you, says the Lord, plans to prosper you and not to harm you, plans to give you hope and a future." The key words in the scripture are *"not to harm you."* There are some people who will act in your best interests, but there are many more who will work to harm you and crush your spirit out of jealousy, resentment, insecurity and their own lack of self-esteem. They do not want you to prosper or have hope for your future.

When you pray and follow God's directions, you will always be true to yourself. You will follow a path that leads to peace and joy. You will have confidence and the blessed assurance that God is in control, and you can trust Him to lead you in the right paths. God will be there for you when all others have abandoned you.

Remember the words of the scriptures this week, and be true to yourself knowing you can trust God's word.

Scriptures:

"Those who know your name will trust in you, for you, Lord, have never forsaken those who seek you." (Psalm 9:10)

"Give thanks to the Lord, for He is good; his love endures forever." (Psalm 118:1)

"For you did not receive a spirit that makes you a slave again to fear..." (Romans 8:15)

"My presence will go with you, and I will give you rest." (Exodus 33:14)

"Those who seek the Lord lack no good thing." (Psalm 34:10b)

Are you being true to yourself? Are you pushing others in a direction that is not best for them?

## -6-
## And the Beat Goes On

Whenever we talk to our elders, the conversation invariably turns to their remembrances of the past and what they call "the good 'ole days." If you listen, it seems as if those times were simpler and less stressful.

There is a rhythm to life. Things are constantly changing everyday, and we sometimes feel as if we are being pulled in many different directions. It seems that many of those changes are negative and not positive. We feel stressed and anxious, tense and uncomfortable. We long for days gone by because somehow we think they were better. We think the rhythm was slower and smoother.

The truth is, life has always been, and will continue to be, a combination of good and bad vibrations. The beat can be slow and steady or fast and erratic. Some days, the smooth, soulful sounds give way to the harshness of heavy metal. Our troubles overwhelm and drown out the peace and joy we seek. When life's trials interfere with your balance, this is the time to give more attention to God. Take time to pray, sing a hymn and give thanks to God for the blessings He has and continues to shower on you. Immerse yourself in God's love for you. His way is smooth and steady.

*Here is a prayer for you:*

Dear God, when the world is too much for me, remind me that you will always comfort and restore me. As I hold on tight to you, give me the courage, strength and wisdom to put life's events in perspective while I continue to walk by faith. Inspire me to live in a positive way that will transform the negatives into something positive. Bring healing, peace and wholeness to me and those I encounter throughout each day as I sing songs of praise and thanksgiving to You. Amen.

How would you describe your rhythm of life?

## -7-
## Make Time for You

Whenever we have a holiday, one thing becomes abundantly clear. We need more rest! We are all overworked and over-stressed. We are forced to work late. We have impossible deadlines to meet and difficult people to work with. We are tired all the time. Even when we have a day off, we cannot rest because we try to squeeze in every activity and chore that we could not get to on the days we were working, or we are worrying about what we have to do when we go back to work. The latest economic survey says that only 57% of the working population takes their full vacation each year.

Your levels of stress increase as the time you allow for rest goes down. Stress wreaks havoc in your life. It can increase your blood pressure to dangerous levels without showing any symptoms. Stress can cause you to lose your temper at the wrong time causing hurt to someone else and/or even yourself. Stress causes you to drive too fast or recklessly because your mind is focused on other things and not the road. Stress keeps you from getting a good night's rest. Stress can affect the way you work. It can cause you to miss deadlines or make costly mistakes. If you are looking for a job, the stress and pressure of the situation can cause you to be frustrated, irritable and disagreeable with the people who are trying to help. And finally, stress can cause you to neglect your loved ones.

You must find a way to make time for you. Make time to relax and periodically get away from the things that are creating so much stress in your life. Have fun with family and friends. Some doctors will tell you to take a short rest now, or face a longer imposed rest in the hospital later.

Rest and reflect on these scriptures, as you make time for you, this week:

"In repentance and rest is your salvation; in quietness and trust is your strength." (Isaiah 30:15b)

"Don't you know that you yourselves are God's temple and that God's Spirit lives in you?" (1 Corinthians 3:16a)

"Come to me, all you who are weary and burdened, and I will give you rest. Take my yoke upon you and learn from me, for I am gentle and humble in heart, and you will find rest for your souls, for my yoke is easy and my burden is light." (Matthew 11:28-30)

"Surely God is my help; the Lord is the one who sustains me." (Psalm 54:4)

"The Lord is my shepherd. I shall not be in want." He makes me lie down in green pastures; he leads me beside quiet waters; he restores my soul." (Psalm 23:1-3a)

Are you doing something to make time for you this week? When did you last take a real vacation?

# -8-
# Imagine What's Possible

Imagination was a driving force in our lives when we were little. We used to imagine that we were movie stars or other famous people. We used to imagine ourselves in our future careers. We imagined living in certain lifestyles – homes, family, friends and social situations.

When I attended a recent convention in Florida, part of the theme was "Imagine What's Possible." As we get older, we tend to put aside our imaginations because we have so much reality to face and deal with everyday, but God still wants you to imagine what's possible.

Here are some things that I imagine:

Imagine what's possible if we trust God more. Proverbs 3:5,6 says, "Trust in the Lord with all your heart and lean not on your own understanding. In all your ways acknowledge Him, and He shall direct your path." If we trust and depend on God, He will direct us to places that we have only imagined.

Imagine what's possible if we pray more. 1 Thessalonians 5:17 says, "Pray continually, give thanks in all circumstances..." Prayer helps us to stay at peace. It gives us strength as we connect with God. Prayer keeps us focused and positive about God's promises to be with us always.

Imagine what's possible if we run to God instead of running away from God. James 4:8 says, "Come near to God, and he will come near to you." "Humble yourselves before the Lord, and he will lift you up." (James 4:10) Whenever we have a problem, many of us think that we can run off and find our own answers to the situations that are causing so much stress and strife. We seek all kinds of solutions before we realize that our help is found with God. When we pray and wait patiently, God will reveal the solutions; He will lead us in the right direction.

Finally, imagine what's possible when we treat people with compassion. Colossians 3:12 says, "Clothe yourselves with compassion, kindness, humility, gentleness and patience." When we show compassion to someone, especially someone who is hurting, we can open the door for them to find peace and wholeness again. We may never know how much a kind word can mean to someone who is lonely or distressed.

"With God all things are possible." (Matthew 19:26b) What do you imagine for your life?

# -9-
# Stop Making Excuses

Do you ever notice, year after year, the relatives, friends and associates who are always giving you excuses for why they cannot do something?  They have many challenges to overcome.  They are trying to find themselves. They have too many things to do.  They are not sure if they can handle anything else. They have to wait until things get better.  They hold onto those excuses as if their lives depend on them.  The people, who tell you those things today, will tell you the same thing a year from now.  Their lives have not moved forward because they continue to allow themselves to be stalled.  They have perfected the art of making excuses.  Eventually, people get tired of them, and then they wonder why no one is calling on them anymore.

You cannot make progress as long as you continue to make excuses.  As long as you allow challenges to control of your life, you will not have access to the blessings of God, and progress will always elude you.  If you are not growing, you are stagnating.  If you are not moving forward, you are moving backward. You must continue to move ahead in spite of the challenges. You must continue to grow and stretch yourself. You have to have faith in God and his promises to you.  If you take one step forward in faith, God will take two for you.  People who have had great success were faced with challenges and obstacles too, but they continued to move forward with positive and exciting things in spite of them. They kept moving even when the odds were against them. They believed that God would make a way.

"You need to persevere so that when you have done the will of God, you will receive what he has promised." (Hebrews 10:36:)

Have you been making excuses to avoid doing some things that you know should be done?

## -10-
## God Will Fight Your Battles

Read the following story in 2 Chronicles, chapter 20 about God's power and might to fight the battles.

"Jehoshaphat was told that a vast army was coming to destroy him and his city. He ordered the people of Judah to fast and come together to seek help from the Lord. At the temple of the Lord, Jehoshaphat prayed to God: "… Power and might are in your hands, and no one can withstand you…. If calamity comes upon us… we will stand in your presence before this temple that bears your Name and will cry out to you in our distress and you will hear us and save us."

The Spirit of the Lord answered him and said, "Do not be afraid or discouraged because of this vast army. For the battle is not yours, but God's… You will not have to fight this battle. Take up your positions; stand firm and see the deliverance the Lord will give you… Do not be afraid; do not be discouraged. Go out to face them tomorrow, and the Lord will be with you."

Jehoshaphat told his people, "Have faith in the Lord your God and you will be upheld; have faith in his prophets and you will be successful." Appointed men went out at the head of the army, saying: "Give thanks to the Lord, for his love endures forever."

As they continued to sing praises, the Lord set ambushes against the armies that were coming against them, and he caused them to destroy each other, and when Jehoshaphat and his army arrived, they found that all of the soldiers were dead. They proceeded to collect all of the supplies and riches that were left. There was so much abundance for them that it took three days for them to collect it."

We must have faith and believe that God will fight our battles. We have to pray and seek deliverance from the forces that come against us. We have to believe in the power of God to change and re-arrange things. Turn your burdens over to God. Wait patiently for the miracles. God will not fail you. Study the scriptures this week:

"I was pushed back and about to fall, but the Lord helped me. The Lord is my strength and my song; he has become my salvation." (Psalm 118:13-14)

"This is the confidence we have in approaching God: that if we ask anything according to his will, he hears us. And if we know that he hears us – whatever we ask, we know that we have what we asked of him." (1 John 5:14-15)

"Have faith in the Lord your God and you will be upheld; have faith in his prophets and you will be successful." (2 Chronicles 20:20c)

"O Lord, my God, I called to you for help and you healed me." (Psalm 30:2)

"For God has delivered me from all my troubles, and my eyes have looked in triumph on my enemies." (Psalm 54:7)

"Cast your cares on the Lord and he will sustain you; he will never let the righteous fall." (Psalm 55:22)

"The Lord is with me; I will not be afraid." (Psalm 118:6)

"So do not fear, for I am with you; do not be dismayed, for I am your God. I will strengthen you and help you." (Isaiah 41:10)

"No one can deliver out of my hand. When I act, who can reverse it?" (Isaiah 43:13b)

"I have told you these things, so that in me you may have peace. In this world you will have trouble, but take heart! I have overcome the world." (John 16:33)

"God is just. He will pay back trouble to those who trouble you and give relief to you who are troubled." (2 Thessalonians 1:6-7)

What battles have you been fighting? Are you willing to turn them over to God?

## -11-
## A Cure for Feelings of Rejection

We have all experienced the pain of rejection at different times in our lives. That rejection may have come from a loved one, a friend, family member and even people on our jobs. It is a very hurtful feeling to open your heart or your soul to someone only to be rejected by thoughts, words and deeds.

Sometimes, we are the perpetrators of the rejection. How many times have we passed judgment or spoken harsh, hurtful words to or about someone. Eventually the information gets back to the person and leads to a hurt that may not be easily reversed.

When we feel rejected by the people in our lives, it can lead to feelings of depression, anxiety, sadness and even guilt. Sometimes people feel guilt because they think they are the cause of the rejection. They don't fit into other people's ideas of what they should be. Feelings of rejection can also lead to isolation. We don't want to be around anyone because we might provoke more rejection.

Jesus experienced the same feelings when he came to be the savior of his people. He was rejected by them.

God's Word is your cure for these feelings. Isaiah 41:9 says, "I have chosen you and have not rejected you." God's love has the power to overcome any feelings of rejection that you may have. God is your comforter and your strength.

Jesus said, "You did not choose me, but I chose you." (John 15:16)

When you are experiencing feelings of rejection, remember, "...we fix our eyes, not on what is seen, but on what is unseen. For what is seen is temporary, but what is unseen is eternal." (2 Corinthians 4:18)

God chooses us because He loves us, and we know that "Love never fails." (1 Corinthians 13:8)

When you need a cure for rejection, read these words and know that God's love will be your comfort, and it will restore your joy.

"Love does not delight in evil but rejoices with the truth. It always protects, always trusts, always hopes, always perseveres." (1 Corinthians 13:6-7)

"And we know that in all things God works for the good of those who love him..." (Romans 8:28a)

"What then shall we say in response to this? If God is for us, who can be against us?" (Romans 8:31)

"...In all these things we are more than conquerors through him who loves us." (Romans 8:37)

Dear God, when I am feeling the pain of rejection, help me to find comfort in You and Your love for me. Amen.

How do you handle feelings of rejection?

# -12-
# Don't Hide Your Light

I attended a recital given by a pastor who had resumed taking piano lessons. Before the pastor began, I read the Bio that was included in the program. It said that he had resumed taking lessons after a 50 year hiatus. I was amazed by his return to something that he obviously loves. I was moved by that brief testimony, and it reminded me of a couple of things.

First, I was immediately transported back to that same period in my life (age 10) when I started taking piano lessons in classical music. I studied for 15 years and became proficient in classical songs. And yet, I have allowed many years to pass without continuing to develop my talent. When people inquire, I simply say, "I don't play anymore!"

Second, it made me wonder how many more people are in the same predicament. You have a personal talent, and yet you have not used it for many years. It may be music, art or some other talent that you began in childhood and gave up in adulthood. Your parents probably forced you into it at first, but now as you think about it, you realize that you really wanted to do it, and you actually miss it.

There are many stories of people who resumed working on something that they gave up many years ago and decided to continue and finish. For example, we see stories about people who went back to college in their

70's, 80's and even their 90's and earned their Bachelors, Masters or Doctoral degrees.

Jesus says, "No one lights a lamp and hides it in a jar or puts it under a bed." (Luke 8:16)

and then, "Let your light so shine before other people that they may see your good works and glorify your Father which is in heaven." (Matthew 5:16)

Don't hide your light. Think about a personal talent that you have, and you have allowed time to make it a distant memory. Take it out of storage, dust it off, and resume the development of that talent. The reward, for your effort, will be priceless!

What talent have you stored away?

## -13-
## Watch What You Say

Whether you are a person of strong faith or a person who believes in universal laws, we are all affected by what we say. How many people experience success when they are constantly professing negative thoughts and feelings? If we keep saying we're going to fail, then we will. If we keep saying that we can't do something, then we won't. With our mouth we turn on the negative or positive force in our lives.

God's words are positive, and His commands are unwavering. Psalm 89:34 says, "I will not violate my covenant or alter what my lips have uttered."

When we are in the midst of a situation, our attitude for success or failure is determined by the words we speak. Keep a journal for 5 days, and make a list of the positive words and negative words that you speak each day. How many times do you say, "I can't" or "Why should I try?" How many times do you speak words of success?

Meditate on these scriptures:

"Thou shall also decree a thing, and it shall be established unto thee." (Job 22:28a (KJV)

"Have faith in the Lord your God, and you will be upheld; have faith in His prophets, and you will be successful." (2 Chronicles 20:20c)

"According to your faith it will be done to you." (Matthew 9:29)

"I tell you the truth, if you have faith as small as a mustard seed, you can say to this mountain, 'Move from here to there' and it will move. Nothing will be impossible for you." (Matthew 17:20)

"Be on your guard; stand firm in the faith; be people of courage; be strong; do everything in love." (1 Corinthians 16:13)

"Jesus said, 'According to your faith will it be done to you." (Matthew 9:29)

How many times do you speak words that are harmful to you?

## -14-
## Change What You Sow; Change What You Reap

Imagine what would happen if a homeowner accidentally planted weeds instead of grass. His lawn would begin to grow and multiply with a crop that would surely choke and kill the grass. We've heard the phrase, "you reap what you sow." What seeds are being sown into your life?

Television news constantly sows seeds of fear, doubt and other negative images into our minds. No matter what time of day you turn on the news, you hear the same stories over and over because they want to influence your thinking in a certain direction. The media will convince you that something is true, when in fact, it is not. They know that constant repetition of their alleged facts will bring the desired results. The goal is to leave you feeling bewildered, confused, anxious and worried about the future.

The same is true of our personal lives. What seeds are you constantly sowing into your own life? Some of us live with fears, doubts, negative thoughts, chaos and confusion everyday. We convince ourselves that the worst is going to happen no matter what we do. Do you notice that people who have negative thoughts always run into bad situations? They live on the dark side of life. Nothing ever goes their way. They think people are always against them. They see all the possibilities of things going wrong. When we constantly sow those negative images and emotions, we are setting ourselves up for a crop that will overwhelm the positive things we should be focused on. Negative emotions will choke and block the blessings that God has ordained for us.

If we believe that God answers pray, and if we believe that God is good, then we must sow seeds of faith everyday. We must sing songs of praise. We must sow seeds with the scriptures, and we must give God the glory and trust that He will give us the victory. We must have total confidence in God and His power to bring us a harvest of blessings.

Luke 8:11b says, "The seed is the word of God." Sow these faith scriptures this week:

"Let love and faithfulness never leave you; bind them around your neck." (Proverbs 3:3)

"The Lord is my light and my salvation...The Lord is the strength of my life." (Psalm 27:1)

"What is impossible with men is possible with God." (Luke 18:27)

"If God is for us, who can be against us?" (Romans 8:31)

"I can do everything through Him who gives me strength." (Philippians 4:13)

"Trust in the Lord forever, for the Lord is the Rock eternal." (Isaiah 26:4)

What seeds are you sowing today to reap a better harvest?

# -15-
# Stand Up to Your Fears

When we are assaulted by situations that cause us to have fears and worries, we want to retreat and hide rather than confront the problems. God has a different plan. He wants us to have the strength and courage to stand up to our fears. We can face them and overcome them with the power that God gives us.

Troubling situations try to take away our power and convince us that we cannot succeed. Our fears lead to more negative feelings: worry, anxiety and stress. These feelings cause your knees to buckle. They make you feel weak and unable to make a step forward. Our fears prevent us from focusing on the blessings that God has for us. Let your faith overcome your fears and trust that God will protect you and give you the victory.

Scriptures:

"Be strong in the Lord and in his mighty power. Put on the full armor of God so that you can take your stand against the devil's schemes." (Ephesians 6:10-11)

"The Lord is on my side. I will not fear. The Lord is on my side. I will not be afraid." (Psalm 118:6 KJV)

"I was pushed back and about to fall, but the Lord helped me. The Lord is my strength and my song; he has become my salvation." (Psalm 118:13-14)

"Then they cried out to the Lord in their trouble, and he brought them out of their distress. (Psalm 107:13)

How do you attack your fears?

# -16-
# Pay Attention

Delia met a very nice man who wanted to share his life with her. He had many wonderful qualities. Delia's friends told her how lucky she was to meet such a wonderful man, but Delia was a drama queen. Every little situation, in her life, took time away from her new beau. When he took her out for dinner, she complained about everything. She was never satisfied with the service or the food.

When they went on vacation, she spent the time complaining about her job and her family. She never listened to his news about his promotion or his plans for the future. She was totally self-absorbed in her life.

Delia hardly noticed, at first, that her beau had almost stopped calling until one of her friends inquired about their relationship. She finally stopped and thought and realized that her beau had disappeared from her life because she had not paid attention to him or their relationship.

When you take your attention away from the positive things and give focus to the negative things, the positive things will begin to fade from your life.

"Be devoted to one another in brotherly love. Honor one another above yourselves." (Romans 12:10)

Are you neglecting anyone in your life? What can you do to change it?

# -17-
# The Power of God

Marie was nervous about her upcoming visit to the doctor. She knew there was a health problem, and she was fearful of the test results. The doctor told her she had a tumor and surgery would be necessary. The procedure was scheduled, and the doctor told her that she may need further treatment after the operation.

Marie was a devoted member of her church. She had strong faith and believed in the power of prayer. She called the prayer warriors and told them her situation. They went to the church and began to pray. They prayed each day until the day of the surgery. Marie put all of her faith and trust in God to bring her through her situation. She continued to pray for a miracle.

When the surgeon took the final x-rays, before the operation, he noticed something unusual. He called in the assistant and the nurse. They looked at the x-ray and decided to redo the tests. They could not believe the results. The tumor was no longer visible. They kept Marie for observation and additional tests, but they could not find any evidence of the tumor. Marie kept praising God for the miracle.

We should never underestimate the power of God to bring the miracles that we seek. Do not panic in the face of problems. Seek God. Call on Him. Have faith and believe.

Study these power scriptures:

"Be still and know that I am God."  (Psalm 46:10)

"I am confident of this: I will see the goodness of the Lord in the land of the living.  Wait on the Lord. Be strong and take heart and wait for the Lord."  (Psalm 27:13-14)

Have you recently experienced the power of God?

# -18-
# Create a Space

If you listen to most interviews with actors, who have been nominated for Awards such as the Oscar or an Emmy, they invariably get around to saying that they are clearing a space on their mantle or bookcase for the award. They are creating a space because they are expecting to receive something new and wonderful. They clear away anything that will clutter the space they have designated.

We are always looking forward to new things. We often go shopping for new clothes or household items only to find that we don't have space for those items because the space is already cluttered with old or outdated items. Some people try to cram the new into the spaces with the old. That often leads to a house full of clutter. We finally realize that we have to clear out the old if we want to make room for the new.

We do the same with our lives. We try to build new relationships on top of the remnants of the old ones. We add layers to cover the hurts. We will not be able to appreciate the new things that want to enter our lives until we create space for them. We have to get rid of the old hurts and disappointments in order to make room for the blessings coming our way.

Remember this scripture:

"No one sews a patch of un-shrunk cloth on an old garment, for the patch will pull away from the garment, making the tear worse. Neither do men/women pour new wine into old wineskins. If they do, the skins will burst, the wine will run out and the wineskins will be ruined." (Matthew 9:16-17)

Are you making space for something new in your life?

# -19-
# Live a Life of Increase

We hear televangelists preaching about prosperity and increase every time we watch one of their shows. They tell you that you are supposed to be wealthy, but all the money in the world will not be enough to give you a prosperous life in God. There are people who are financially secure and yet, all of their money is not enough when they face a life-threatening illness.

Living a life of increase does not necessarily mean monetary gain. We live a life of increase when we grow in knowledge, wisdom, courage and strength. When you continue your education to pursue new degrees and certificates, you are living a life of increase. We live a life of increase when we show compassion to people. We live a life of increase when we grow spiritually. We live a life of increase when we grow in faith.

"Instruct a wise person and he/she will be wiser still; teach a righteous person and he/she will add to his/her learning." (Proverbs 9:9)

"Many will go here and there to increase knowledge." (Daniel 12:4b)

How would you determine if you are living a life of increase?

# -20-
# What is Haunting You?

When we hear the word "haunted," we usually think about the horror movies where houses are haunted by spirits and demons from past generations. The characters spend their time running away from and trying to defeat the things that are haunting them.

People can be haunted by something that continues to linger in their minds from years past. It causes them to be stuck. It torments them. It affects everything that they do in the present. Before you can move forward with your life, you have to stop and figure out what is haunting you.

Reflect on this Story:

When Emily was in her early twenties, she began her teaching career. She was very much in love with her boyfriend. After she rented her first apartment, her boyfriend suddenly broke up with her. Emily was devastated. It took many months for her to get over the hurt and disappointment. During that period in her life, she was very critical of everyone. She felt betrayed and also guilty because she felt that she did something to drive the person away from her.

Even though she moved on to other relationships, she was haunted by the memories of that first relationship. She, subconsciously, believed other men would treat her the same way, so she sabotaged the relationships before they had a chance to hurt her. One day, she met some-one who really took the time to understand her behav-ior. He helped her to uncover what had been haunting her about that past relationship. When she finally felt comfortable to talk about it, she was able to release the hurt and the feelings of guilt. She was able to under-stand her behavior and why she reacted in certain ways. She was free to move on.

"Forget the former things. Do not dwell on the past." (Isaiah 43:18)

Is something in your past affecting you in a negative way? Find a way to talk about it, and then, let it go. Free yourself from what is haunting you.

# -21-
# The Walls are Coming Down

We are sometimes surrounded by the emotions resulting from our troubles. They are like walls that keep building up all around us. One side is a wall of fear. Fear keeps growing every time we stop trusting God. One wall is worry. We constantly worry about every situation, real and imagined. One wall is doubt. We doubt God's ability to bring us through our situations. The fourth wall is frustration. We become frustrated when we can't turn a situation around on our own. These walls keep growing higher and higher, and then they begin to close in on us. They begin to squeeze the life out of us. We feel powerless.

There is a weapon that will break through those walls. The walls will come tumbling down when we begin to trust and rely on God. The walls will come tumbling down when we have faith and pray.

In the Book of Joshua, Joshua did not believe that he and his soldiers could take the city of Jericho. The walls were high and strong. God had already planned the victory. He told Joshua that the city would be theirs. They had to follow a plan for seven days, and then on the final day, they would shout and the walls of Jericho would come down. They took the city and all of the treasures because Joshua trusted God.

If you trust God, believe in His promises and have faith, your walls will come down.

What represents the walls in your life?

# -22-
# Don't Give Up - It's Just a Matter of Time

Our personal lives can sometimes become an unending series of troubles, trials and tests. No matter what we do, our situations continue to plague us. We are living with fears, doubts and worries. As we struggle to overcome one situation, another problem comes to take its place. We don't see a light at the end of the tunnel. We've cried and prayed, and yet nothing has changed. We begin to wonder if our lives will ever get better.

Negative emotions control your minds. Fear tries to destroy your optimism. Fear works to convince you that you will not win over your challenges. Fear tries to make you withdraw and hide. Fear fuels your anxiety. Fear will cause you to feel discouraged and depressed.

There is a saying that tells you the night is darkest just before the dawn. Your negative emotions prevent you from seeing that there is a way out. You may be in the darkest part of your life, but God does not want you to give up. He is working to bring the miracles. He is working to turn your situation around. God is working to change your circumstances. You may not see any evidence of the change that is coming, but God says your faith will bring you through the trials. God tells you to believe and don't doubt. Remember what God has done for you in the past.

Maintain and strengthen your faith. Stay in prayer. Read the scriptures for reinforcement every time you begin to doubt. Sing a song. There is a gospel hymn that says, "I don't feel no ways tired. Nobody told me the road would be easy; I don't believe he brought me this far to leave me." God has not left you. He has not given up on you. He will bring the healing. He will change your circumstances. He will restore your joy. He will bring the blessings. He will give you the victory.

Your problems may seem insurmountable, but keep looking to God. He says don't give up one minute before your miracle. Your victory is closer than you think. Stay focused on God's love for you, and wait patiently for the miracles. Pray, sing a song and keep moving forward. It's just a matter of time. It may not be in the time you have set, but God's time is not our time. His way is not our way, but His plan is certain. Wait for God to move in your life, and don't give up.

This week, be strengthened by these scriptures:

"Blessed is the person who perseveres under trial, because when they have stood the test, they will receive the crown of life that God has promised to those who love him." (James 1:12)

"Stand firm. Let nothing move you. Always give yourselves fully to the work of the Lord, because you know that your labor in the Lord is not in vain." (1 Corinthians 15:58)

"Perseverance must finish its work so that you may be mature and complete, not lacking anything." (James 1:4-5)

"Let us not become weary in doing good, for at the proper time, we will reap a harvest if we do not give up." (Galatians 6:9)

"God will deliver the needy who cry out, the afflicted who have no one to help." (Psalm 72:12)

What do you want to change in your life? Are you trusting God to bring the changes that you seek?

## -23-
## You Can Overcome

Life is a series of ups and downs. When we are in the down times, we can be overwhelmed with fears, worries and doubts. We may feel that a negative situation has pushed all of the hope far away beyond our grasp. We feel like the dark is going to last forever.

There are a few things we should remember and believe:

1. God will not give us more than we can bear.

2. We have the strength deep inside us.

3. The sun will shine again.

4. We can overcome every problem when God is part of the plan.

5. God will always understand and feel our pain.

6. God's love will never fail.

7. God's faithfulness is enough to bring us through.

8. Prayer changes things.

9. There are people in our lives who will always love us unconditionally.

10. God is our protector.

"For I am the Lord, your God, who takes hold of your right hand and says to you, Do not fear, I will help you." (Isaiah 41:13)

Do you trust God to help you overcome? How do you demonstrate that trust?

# -24-
# A Friend in Your Exile

Have you ever been lost in an exile experience? So many things are going wrong with your life that you don't know which way to turn. You pray everyday, but God has not answered. Your faith begins to get weak because you believe that God has abandoned you. You want to give up on life. You may even feel like running away.

God has not left you. He is there with you in the exile experiences. He knows what you need, and He is working a plan for your relief.

In 1 Kings 17, verses 7-16, the prophet Elijah met a widow who was gathering sticks. He asked the widow for some water and bread. She had very little. She had planned to make one last meal for herself and her son. She knew that they were about to starve to death. Elijah said to her, "Don't be afraid." He told her to make a small cake of bread for him and then go home and make her meal. He told her that the jar of flour would not be used up and the jug of oil would not run dry. It was as he said. She did not run out of anything. She had been blessed to come out of her famine.

God is doing the same thing for you. There are blessings that will continue to flow into your life if you have faith and believe while you are in your exile. God is looking for you right now.

Strengthen your faith with these scriptures:

"Have faith in the Lord your God and you will be upheld; have faith in his prophets, and you will be successful." (2 Chronicles 20:20b)

"I will search for the lost and bring back the strays. I will bind up the injured and strengthen the weak." (Ezekiel 34:16a)

When you are deep in exile, don't give up on God. Stay strong in your faith and know that God is searching for you, and He will bring you out to receive your abundant blessings.

Do you sometimes feel as if you are in an exile from life? What is causing your exile?

# -25-
# The Fruit of the Spirit

"The fruit of the spirit is love, joy, peace, patience, kindness, goodness, faithfulness, gentleness and self-control." (Galations 5:22)

Living by the fruit of the spirit helps us to have the life that God wants for us, but when we live the opposite of these fruits, we will forever have internal and external conflicts. We will be controlled by fear, worry, anxiety and selfishness. We will walk in the path that takes us away from God and His blessings for our lives. We will invite the negative spirits to control our thoughts and actions. We will walk in the path of darkness instead of walking in God's light.

If you are living by the fruits of the spirit, you will be kind to people. You will show compassion to those who reach out to you. You will take the time to make a phone call to someone who has been sick, living alone or mourning over the death of a loved one. You will take the time to visit or do something nice without looking for recognition of your actions. You will take time to understand and share your wisdom with others.

When you live by the fruits of the spirit, God will bless your life. Ecclesiastes says, "Cast your bread upon the waters, for after many days, you will find it again." (Ecclesiastes 11:1) When you show kindness and compassion, patience and goodness, those fruits will be returned to you. You will be blessed with an abundance of peace, love and joy because God is faithful to those who delight in His ways.

Meditate on this modern version of the scripture from 1 Corinthians 12:4-11, and you will begin to know peace that the world can't give or take away from you. You will have love in your heart and joy in your soul.

"There are different kinds of spiritual gifts, but the same Spirit gives them. There are different ways of serving, but the same God gives the ability to everyone for their particular service. The Spirit's presence is shown in some way in each person for the good of all. The Spirit gives one person a message full of wisdom, while to another person, the same Spirit gives a message full of knowledge. One and the same Spirit gives faith to one person, while another person, receives the power to heal. The Spirit gives one person the power to work miracles; to another, the gift of speaking God's message; and to yet another, the ability to tell the difference between gifts that come from the Spirit and those that do not... but it is one and the same Spirit who does all this; as he wishes; he gives a different gift to each person."

Are you living your life by the fruits of the spirit?

# -26-
# It's Your Mood, Not Your Life

Have you ever started your day in a good mood, and then someone says something to you that sets you off and puts you in a bad mood? It happens to all of us. We may not even remember what caused us to be in a terrible mood. We just know that we have entered into a dark abyss, and whatever or whoever enters our space is subjected to the negativity that surrounds us.

Bad moods create negative energy. During those times, nothing is right. We don't like the way we look or feel. We are easily offended by anything that is said to us. We argue with people who may be trying to help or make suggestions. We take everything the wrong way. We don't like ourselves, and we definitely don't like other people. The entire world seems off balance. When we speak, we hurt and offend people. They get on every nerve-- some we didn't even know we had. You probably want to wear a sign that says, "Don't talk to me. I'm in a bad mood!"

As emotional, feeling people, we have to accept that our moods are always changing. You can't avoid them, and you can't control them. It is important to be aware in order to minimize the damage that your mood can cause. When people are in a low mood, they feel the need to set people straight. It's the time when you want to make decisions even though they may not be the right ones. You become defensive, hostile and stubborn. You may break up with someone you love. In extreme cases, you may quit your job or leave home. All of your reason, knowledge and wisdom goes out the window.

It is, however, important to recognize that your moods are just that - moods. They are temporary, and they do not define your life or who you are. A low mood will change as suddenly as it came upon you. You may see something funny or watch a comedy on television that really makes you laugh. Something really nice may happen to put a smile on your face. Just as suddenly as the bad mood came, it disappears.

Minimize the damage when you are in a low mood. Acknowledge your mood, and accept that it is temporary. Low moods distort your thinking. Don't trust your judgment. Do not make any important decisions. Stop listening to the negative thoughts going around in your mind. Do not engage in arguments. Do things that will take your mind off yourself for a while. Read, pray and spend some time in meditation. Most of all, give yourself time. Your mood will change, and once again, you will see the beauty of life and living. Balance will be restored. Remember, it's a mood, not your life. Be blessed to know that God does not change.

"Every good and perfect gift is from above, coming down from the Father of the heavenly lights, who does not change like shifting shadows." (James 1:17)

"The Lord is good to all; He has compassion on all He has made." (Psalm 145:9)

What kind of decisions have you made when you were in a bad mood? Were you sorry after your mood changed?

## -27-
## God Always Comes to the Rescue

I was talking to a friend recently who is having trouble with his knee. He has been advised to have surgery as soon as possible to correct the situation. He told me that the pain has become increasingly unbearable, especially at night. It has affected his ability to climb stairs or go to work everyday. He told me about a night recently that was a real test of his faith. He woke up with severe pain, pain that would not go away no matter what he did. It reached a level that was unbearable, and all he could do was pray. He cried out and told God that he could not take the pain any longer, and he needed relief right now. Within 10 minutes, the pain had subsided, and he was able to go back to sleep and rest all night without any more discomfort. It was his testimony that God answers pray and comes when you need Him.

This is not the first time I've heard testimonies about God's power to change things or bring relief right away. God knows how much we can bear when we are in extreme distress. He does not want us to suffer. He will come to the rescue at the right time. He will bring relief from the pain, from the hurts and from the heartaches. We are God's children, and He will never abandon us.

The Psalmist gives us the words of assurance that we need:

"Praise the Lord, O my soul, and forget not all his benefits – who forgives your sins and heals all your diseases." (Psalm 103:2-3)

"Be still and know that I am God." (Psalm 46:10)

"The Lord is my strength and my shield; my heart trusts in him, and I am helped." (Psalm 28:7)

"Weeping may remain for a night, but rejoicing comes in the morning." (Psalm 30:5)

"The Lord is my strength and my shield; my heart trusts in him, and I am helped." (Psalm 28:7)

"O Lord, my God, I called to you for help and you healed me." (Psalm 30:2)

"Answer me when I call to you, O my righteous God. Give me relief from my distress; be merciful to me and hear my prayer." (Psalm 4:1)

God will not forsake you or leave you alone. He will come to the rescue. Have faith and trust; pray and believe. Your prayers will be answered.

Do you need relief from your suffering? Have you asked God in faith, believing that He is able?

## -28-
## Five Things That Block the
## Flow of Your Blessings

You pray, attend worship services, read the Bible, and yet the blessings that you seek are not flowing into your life. You feel that God has abandoned you in your time of need, but the truth is, He is trying to reach you. The problem is a human one. You are blocking God's blessings because you are consumed and controlled by negative emotions: Fear, worry, doubt, anger and depression. If you cannot let go of these blessing blockers, you will not be in a position to receive God's grace.

Fear keeps us from believing that God is able. You can conquer your fear. It does not have to control you.

*Romans 8:15 "For you did not receive a spirit that makes you a slave again to fear, but you received the Spirit of sonship, and by him we cry, "Abba," Father."*

*Psalm 91:9-11 "If you make the Most High your dwelling, even the Lord, who is my refuge, then no harm will befall you, no disaster will come near your tent, for he will command his angels concerning you to guard you in all your ways."*

Worry keeps us focused on all of the potential negative outcomes instead of trusting God to take care of our needs. His word says,

*Philippians 4:6-7*

*"Do not be anxious about anything, but in everything, by prayer and petition, with thanksgiving, present your requests to God. And the peace of God, which transcends all understanding, will guard your hearts and your minds."*

*Psalm 4:1 "Answer me when I call to you, O righteous God. Give me relief from my distress; be merciful to me and hear my prayer."*

Doubt prevents us from having faith in God's word. You can overcome doubt if you remember,

*Mark 11:24 "Therefore, I tell you, whatever you ask for in prayer, believe that you have received it, and it will be yours."*

*Psalm 18:30 "As for God, his way is perfect; the word of the Lord is flawless. He is a shield for all who take refuge in him."*

Anger keeps us focused on negative energy. It creates more negative feelings.

*Psalm 37:8 "Refrain from anger and turn from wrath; do not fret – it leads only to evil."*

*Matthew 6:14 "For if you forgive men when they sin against you, your heavenly Father will also forgive you."*

Depression makes us feel hopeless. It tells us to give up on God.

*Psalm 34:17-18 "The righteous cry out, and the Lord hears them; he delivers them from all their troubles. The Lord is close to the brokenhearted and saves those who are crushed in spirit."*

*Isaiah 41:10b "Do not be dismayed, for I am your God. I will strengthen you and help you. I will uphold you with my righteous right hand."*

God's promises are eternal and certain if you don't allow the blessing blockers to gain a stronghold in your mind. God's word will manifest in your lives. Hold onto your faith. Stay consistent in your prayers. Trust God and believe in his transforming power. Overcome your negative emotions with the positive promises of God, and you will experience showers of blessings in your life.

What blocks your blessings?

# -29-
# Habits Cannot Change Themselves

We all have habits that we are unhappy with. We may want to...

o Lose weight, but we continue to eat too much of the wrong foods;

o Stop smoking, but we need those cigarettes to get us through the stressful days;

o Start exercising, but we are too tired at the end of the day, and there's a special show on cable that we don't want to miss;

o Stop drinking or using drugs, but we need to ease our emotional pains;

o Stop gambling, but one more bet might be the one to help us recoup all of the money we have lost in the past.

There are many other bad habits that are too lengthy to list here.

We are victims and martyrs in our suffering. Bad habits control our lives and leave us feeling helpless. They keep us in bondage. We want these habits to change and go away, but one fact is clear. Unless we do something positive to change our bad habits, they will continue to torture us.  We will always feel guilt and remorse because we are not giving the best to ourselves.

The inner turmoil that we experience is our higher self telling us that we don't have to live on the dark side of life.  W can do better and be better.

Many years ago, my mother was a pack a day smoker.  She had tried many times to stop but was unsuccessful.  One of her cousins was in the hospital suffering from cancer which had spread from his lungs to his brain in a short time.  As he lay there in pain, my mother remembered that he was a chain smoker.  When she went to church the next Sunday, during the altar call, she brought her pack of cigarettes and placed them on the altar.  She asked God to touch her and take the taste and desire for cigarettes away from her.  She got up from the altar and never took another puff.  She never suffered any setbacks.  She had been freed because she took one step toward God and had faith in his grace and mercy.

God wants you to know that you are not alone in your struggles because He sees and understands the suffering.  The beginning of change comes with one step in faith toward God.  With one step, you will activate God's grace and mercy.  He will give you the courage to take action as He reveals His plan to you.

"Let us then approach the throne of grace with confidence, so that we may receive mercy and find grace to help us in our time of need."  (Hebrews 4:16)

# Section Four: Scriptures for Daily Meditation and Reflection

The Bible is the place to go for knowledge, understanding, wisdom and strength. Through God's Word, you can find the weapons that will give you the victory in every situation. Put on the full armor of God.

**The Bible will give you the victory when you feel...**

**Discouraged:**
John 14:1
"Do not let your hearts be troubled. Trust in God; also trust in me."

Psalm 183:7
"Though I walk in the midst of trouble, you preserve my life."

Psalm 27:1-2
"The Lord is my light and my salvation. Whom shall I fear? The Lord is the stronghold of my life. Of whom shall I be afraid?"

Isaiah 41:13
"For I am the Lord, your God, who takes hold of your right hand and says to you, 'Do not fear; I will help you."

Psalm 19:7
"The law of the Lord is perfect, reviving the soul."

**Worried:**
1 Peter 5:7
"Cast all your anxiety on him because he cares for you."

Philippians 4:6,7
"Do not be anxious about anything, but in everything, by prayer and petition, with thanksgiving, present your requests to God. And the peace of God which transcends all understanding, will guard your hearts and your minds."

Colossians 3:15
"Let the peace of God rule in your hearts and minds."

Psalm 4:8
"I will lie down and sleep in peace, for you alone, O Lord, make me dwell in safety."

Philippians 4:19
"And my God will meet all your needs according to his glorious riches."

**Dissatisfied:**
Philippians 4:12.13

"I know what it is to be in need, and I know what it is to have plenty. I have learned the secret of being content in any and every situation, whether well fed or hungry, whether living in plenty or in want. I can do everything through him who gives me strength."

Psalm 37:3,4
"Trust in the Lord and do good; dwell in the land and enjoy safe pasture. Delight yourself in the Lord, and he will give you the desires of your heart."

Psalm 107:8,9
"Let them give thanks to the Lord for his unfailing love and his wonderful deeds for people, for he satisfies the thirsty and fills the hungry with good things."

**Lonely:**
Psalm 147:3
"He heals the brokenhearted and binds up their wounds."

Psalm 147:11
"The Lord delights in those who fear him, who put their hope in his unfailing love."

Psalm 27:10
"Though my father and mother forsake me, the Lord will receive me."

Psalm 34:18
"The Lord is close to the brokenhearted and saves those who are crushed in spirit."

**Confused:**
Psalm 32:8
"I will instruct you and teach you in the way you should go. I will counsel you and watch over you."

1 Corinthians 14:33
"For God is not a God of disorder but of peace."

James 1:5
"If any of you lacks wisdom, he should ask God, who gives generously to all without finding fault."

2 Timothy 1:7
"For God did not give us a spirit of timidity, but a spirit of power, of love and of self-discipline."

Proverbs 3:5,6
"Trust in the Lord with all your heart and lean not on your own understanding; in all your ways acknowledge him, and he will make your paths straight."

**Depressed:**
Psalm 34:18
"The Lord is close to the brokenhearted and saves those who are crushed in spirit."

Psalm 30:5b
"Weeping may endure for a night, but rejoicing comes in the morning."

Psalm 55:22
"Cast all your cares on the Lord, and he will sustain you; he will never let the righteous fall."

## The Bible will give you the victory when you have...
## Faith

Hebrews 11:1
"Now faith is being sure of what we hope for and certain of what we do not see."

Hebrews 11:6
"And without faith, it is impossible to please God, because anyone who comes to him must believe that he exists and that he rewards those who earnestly seek him."

Mark 9:23
"Therefore I tell you, whatever you ask for in prayer, believe that you have received it, and it will be yours."

Romans 10:17
"Consequently, faith comes from hearing the message, and the message is heard through the word of God."

James 5:15
"And the prayer offered in faith will make the sick person well; the Lord will raise them up. If they have sinned, they will be forgiven."

### Confidence:
Hebrews 10:35,36
"So do not throw away your confidence; it will be richly rewarded. You need to persevere so that when you have done the will of God, you will receive what he has promised."

Philippians 1:6
"Now being confident of this, that he who began a good work in you will carry it on to completion."

Matthew 6:33
"But seek first the kingdom of God and his righteousness and all these things will be given to you as well."

Proverbs 3:26
"For the Lord will be your confidence and will keep your foot from being snared."

Romans 8:37
"In all these things, we are more than conquerors through him who loves us."

**Strength:**
Isaiah 40:31
"But those who hope in the Lord will renew their strength. They will soar on wings like eagles; they will run and not grow weary; they will walk and not be faint."

2 Samuel 22:33
"It is God who arms me with strength and makes my way perfect."

Psalm 28:7
"The Lord is my strength and my shield; my heart trusts in him, and I am helped."

Deuteronomy 31:6

"Be strong and courageous. Do not be afraid or terrified...for the Lord, your God, goes with you; he will never leave nor forsake you."

## Hope:
Isaiah 43:2
"When you pass through the waters, I will be with you, and when you pass through the rivers they will not sweep over you. When you walk through the fire, you will not be burned; the flames will not set you ablaze."

Jeremiah 32:27
"I am the Lord, the God of all mankind. Is anything too hard for me?"

Luke 1:37
"For nothing is impossible with God."

Psalm 130:5
"I wait for the Lord, my soul waits, and in his word I put my hope."

## Understanding:
Psalm 111:10
The fear of the Lord is the beginning of wisdom; all who follow his precepts have good understanding."

Proverbs 16:16
How much better to get wisdom than gold, to choose understanding rather than silver."

Proverbs 23:23b

"Get wisdom, discipline and understanding."

Proverbs 4:7
"Wisdom is supreme; therefore get wisdom.  Though it cost all you have, get understanding."

**Love**
1 John 4:7

"Dear friends, let us love one another, for love comes from God.  Everyone who loves has been born of God and knows God."

1 John 4:12
"No one has ever seen God; but if we love one another, God lives in us and his love is made complete in us."

Deuteronomy 30:20
"Love the Lord your God, listen to his voice, and hold fast to him, for the Lord is your life."

**When you need God's Intervention...**
Psalm 46:10  "Be still and know that I am God."
Proverbs 3:5,6

"Trust in the Lord with all your heart, and lean not on your own understanding.  In all your ways acknowledge him, and he shall direct your paths."

1 Thessalonians 5:16,17
Be joyful always; pray continually; give thanks in all circumstances."

2 Thessalonians 1:6,7
"God is just: He will pay back trouble to those who trouble you and give relief to you who are troubled."

Romans 8:28, 31

"And we know that in all things God works for the good of those who love him." "If God is for us, who can be against us?"

# About the Author

Louise is a living testament of her writings because she is an inspiration. In 2002, with her first published book, *Inspirations for the Heart and Soul,* Louise touched audiences with the friendly-familiar format of simple letters containing affirmations, scripture and divine inspirations which encourages readers to begin a walk with God based on simple faith in the One whose love for us is deeper than we can think or imagine. In her second book, *Our Strength Comes from God,* published in December, 2003, Louise invites an even larger audience of readers to explore a deeper relationship with God. Relying on a variety of scriptures, the letters and affirmations detailed are designed to help people in their desire to cope with and overcome life's trials and challenges. Her third book *Faith for All Seasons,* compels the reader to become more intimate with God through daily/weekly devotionals, prayers, journaling and Bible study. The theological premise underlying the creation of this book is: *"Have faith in God's process in every season, and the best of life will be yours."* Her fourth book, *Faith to Overcome,* moves readers to a time of quiet reflection with the devotionals, scriptures and prayers contained within its pages. Her fifth work, ***Inspirations from God,*** continues the journey with meditations, prayers and scriptures. These books of inspiration, written by one who is indeed inspired by God like the saints of old, can be purchased on Amazon.com and are also available through Kindle.

You can stay up to date on the latest inspirations and learn more about each of these 5 books by visiting and registering on the web site: www.myinspirationsfromgod.com